WOKA MAN

FOSTERING THROUGH THE EYES OF A CHILD — VOLUME 2

WOKA MAN

TRAPPED IN A LIFE OF COERCION AND DECEPTION

DESMOND TOMLINSON

MANGIFERA
BLOOM
Port St Lucie

Published by Mangifera Bloom, Port St Lucie

Find out more at https://www.fosteringthroughtheeyesofachild.net

1st Edition

ISBN: 978-1-7342500-1-5 (Paperback)
ISBN: 978-1-7342500-5-3 (ebook)

Library of Congress Control Number: 2020909335

Edited by Mikel Benton
Cover illustration by Michael Rohani
Book design by DesignForBooks.com

Printed in the U.S.A.

CONTENTS

THE EXORDIUM   IX

Dedication   ix

How My Autobiography Is Organized   xi

Conventions Used   xiii

Additional Content   xiv

ACKNOWLEDGMENT AND OVERVIEW   XV

Overview   xv

Acknowledgment   xvi

CHAPTER 1   THE ELUSIVENESS OF A SUPERFICIAL APPEARANCE   1

The Prodigious Illusion   1

The Never-ending Upheaval   2

The Dawn of a New Day   10

Who Are These Girls, and Why Are They Here?   23

The Anticipated Drama   24

The Relentless Mocking of My Soles   30

CHAPTER 2   PARENTING PHILOSOPHIES   35

All Good Things Have Come to an End   35

Up the Ante   43

Devious Encounters   54

Beating Apparatus   72

Stringent Cost-saving Measures 82

CHAPTER 3 THE UNRAVELLING 87

Barry's Untimely Departure 87
Narrowly Escaping the Colossal Bangarang 91

CHAPTER 4 EXTENDING THE FAMILY 93

CHAPTER 5 THE RETURN OF THE FOSTER CHILD 97

CHAPTER 6 ARRIVALS AND DEPARTURES 99

Adding Three Johnsons to the Family 99
Let's Just Add One More Person to the Family 100
Phillip's Departure 102
Let's Make Room for One More Foster Child 104
The Abrupt Departure of the Johnsons 106
Foster Children Academic Progress 114
More Money, More Work 119

CHAPTER 7 RESISTING THE UNACCEPTABLE 123

CHAPTER 8 THE ETERNAL, PHYSICAL, AND EMOTIONAL SEPARATION 129

CHAPTER 9 THE AFTERMATH 135

Adopted Children Sent off to Boarding School 135
Makeshift Grocery Store 136
Adding Two More Children to the Drama House 144
Jacqueline's Departure 147
Adding a Helping Hand 154
The Bandit 159

Contents

Being at the Wrong Place at the Wrong Time   164

CHAPTER **10** THE OMEGA (Ω)   171

Applying My Brother's Rationale   171

Seeking Refuge   175

The Inevitable   177

Being Shuttled into the Great Unknown   179

Back in the Hands of the Child Development Agency   179

JAMAICA – THE JOURNEY   187

APPENDIX **A** PREDATED AND POSTDATED ERAS OF THE FOSTER CARE SYSTEM   189

Unintended Consequences of the Foster Care System   192

APPENDIX **B** A PAINFUL LESSON   197

APPENDIX **C** JAMAICAN, ACADEMIC LEVELS, PROGRESS, AND INSTITUTIONS   201

REFERENCES   203

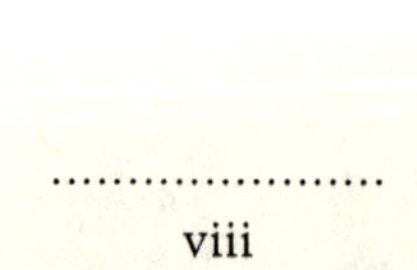

THE EXORDIUM

Dedication

First and foremost, I would like to give God the glory for bestowing unto me health, strength, happiness, and the many other wonderful blessings of life. Second, I would like to dedicate this volume to all children who have suffered abuse. Finally, in honor of my brother's memories, I have entitled this volume as Woka Man. The history surrounding the Woka Man label has been documented in volume 4 of my autobiography.

I would like to commence by highlighting two of the more pressing questions that I keep pondering over since the day I decided to share my life story. The first is, what defining message will my life experiences convey to humanity as a whole? And second, will humanity be receptive to such a message? I thought I had these questions all figured out, but the more I think about them, the more I realize that I may never be able to come up with definitive answers. However, in my quest to uncover the answers, I would hope that you join me as I traverse the emotional, at times the roller-coaster-like, journey of my life. At one point, I thought about the possibility of conveying my story verbally. On second thought, I realized that this method would certainly not be the most effective. With that in mind, I set out to tell my story in a written form and hope to accomplish the following:

- To highlight the wonderful blessings of God that have transformed my life

- To establish the fact that life is not just about my inner circle or me, but also about individuals who have not been fortunate to be loved and cared for, especially throughout their early childhood and adolescent years

- To acknowledge and credit the many individuals and institutions that have provided me with the help and support I desperately needed throughout my early childhood years.

- To highlight the fact that the desire to pray and the need to persevere are the two most important characteristics that I relied on each day to overcome life's obstacles[1]

- To shine a light on the foster care system and stress the need for us to develop and implement policies to protect children and the less fortunate

- To share my personal experiences that have allowed me to realize the undeniable parallel between my former foster parents' actions and our actions today[2]

---

1 Although I have intentionally left out tangible aspects such as financial needs, it does not mean that I do not value their importance. However, the point I am conveying is this: financial and other material possessions are not characteristics of one's being. I have highlighted this concept in detail, especially throughout the compare-and-contrast sections dealing with Aunt Lucy and my former foster parents. This will become apparent in volume 3 of my autobiography.

2 The most obvious are those perpetrated by deception, and the utter disregard for the well-being of others, especially the less fortunate. I also use this

- To provide inspiration and comfort to all, particularly the less fortunate (orphans) who have gone through or find themselves going through challenging times

How My Autobiography Is Organized

My autobiography is presented in four volumes. The first three volumes cover the unpredictable, life-changing events that occurred while I was living on the tropical island of Jamaica. The fourth reflects the transformational journey of my life after I migrated to the United States of America.

Volume 1, *The Separation* – this volume takes into account the following:

- Life with my father
- The emotional separation when my brother and I were forcefully removed from our father's care and transferred to an orphanage
- The joyous reunification when my brother and I were transferred from the orphanage back to our father's care
- The emotional separation when my brother, my sisters, and I were forcefully removed from our father's care and divvied up between orphanages
- The transfer of my brother and me from the orphanage to our mother's care

---

opportunity to highlight my brother's relentless cry for justice, and the need to challenge hearts and minds to pursue justice and peace above ego, self-acclaimed interests, and conflicts.

- The emotional separation when my brother and I were forcefully removed from our mother's care and returned to the orphanage

Volume 2, *Woka Man* – this volume takes into account the following:

- The transfer of my brother and me from the orphanage to a foster home
- The eternal, physical, and emotional separation that occurred when my brother was transferred to a correctional institution
- The remaining time I spent with my foster parents, including how, when, and why I was also removed from their care

Volume 3, *The Turning Point* – this volume takes into account the following:

- The transition to and from a temporary foster home
- When and how I was united with my wonderful, caring, loving foster mother, Aunt Lucy
- Reunion with my biological family, including my only brother
- The continuation of my academic, professional, social, and *spiritual* journey

Volume 4, *A Dream Come True* – this volume takes into account the following:

- The remaining precious and unforgettable time I spent with my wonderful, caring, loving foster mother, Aunt Lucy

- The journey to a land far, far away to fulfill my academic dream

- The unimaginable but inspiring and transformative academic, professional, social, and *spiritual* opportunities that continue to shape and reshape my life

- The miraculous birth of life and the family of a lifetime

Conventions Used

To maintain the originality of individual quotes, phrases, and humor, I have incorporated the Jamaican Patois (Patwa) along with the English translations. However, in some cases, I have paraphrased both the Jamaican Patois and English translations as a way to maintain contextuality. Please bear in mind that the Jamaican Patois does not have a definitive structure. Therefore, the spelling and pronunciation of certain words could differ slightly. There are many sources and variations; however, I have relied on the *Jabari Authentic Jamaican Dictionary of the Jamic Language* as a guide (Reynolds 2006).

Although this book is my autobiography, I have taken the initiative to highlight the many acts of kindness bestowed unto me by family members, friends, acquaintances, strangers, and prominent institutions. These individuals and institutions are the many parts that have made my life whole. They have provided me with life's essentials and more. I have also been blessed to have received a lifetime of spiritual and moral support that has guided my actions and the way I perceive my fellow humankind.

Initially, I thought about composing my life story to include only the wonderful events; however, I was reminded that omitting the more painful memories would certainly not reflect an accurate picture of my life. Therefore, to convey the full story and to put everything into perspective, I have decided to highlight the unfortunate situations as well.

Irrespective of the many unfortunate circumstances, especially those concerning my only brother, I do hope that you will enjoy a smile and a little laughter as you read my tidbits of humor. I must also warn you that a number of my witticisms might go, swoosh, right over your head because they might be technologically funneled or skewed to a particular culture or era; or in the words of a teenager, they might come across as lame or botched. For the humor that you do not have a clue about, you are just going to have to wave the Google magic wand for further clarification.

Additional Content

To complement my written autobiography, I have created the www.fosteringthroughtheeyesofachild.net website to provide additional information and content, such as pictures and links for the subjects and topics that I have referred to throughout the different volumes. Also, the reader or interested party is more than welcome to use this website to provide an ongoing discussion regarding the content of my autobiography and other topics associated with the development and well-being of children.

ACKNOWLEDGMENT AND OVERVIEW

Overview

Please bear with me while I take this opportunity to provide you with a brief update of my siblings, Paulette, Pauline and George Tomlinson. Throughout the early stages of our childhood, Paulette, Pauline, George, and I were living exclusively with our father and adhering to his interpretation of the Rastafarian doctrines. After many years of not being allowed to attend school, the Child Development Agency (CDA) took us from our father's care and placed us in different orphanages. Pauline and Paulette were transferred among different orphanages over many years before they were finally reunited with our elder sisters, Eupheme (Inez) and Grace Tomlinson. The details of this reunion are covered in volume 3.

George and I experienced a roller-coaster-like, back-and-forth transition between our father, the orphanage, and our mother's care. After several years of back and forth between our parents and the orphanage, the CDA finally transferred us to a foster home. Instead of receiving the love and care we desperately needed, however, we were abused physically and psychologically by our foster parents. My brother made several unsuccessful attempts to reason with our foster parents for basic fairness and to let them (more so our foster mother) know that we deserved to be treated like human beings. In return, my brother was severely punished by our foster mother because she considered his outspokenness presumptuous and ill-mannered. Not only that, but she detested his very presence. In the end, they took my brother to a juvenile correctional institution without any justification other than his relentless cry for justice.

Acknowledgment

Finally, I would like to extend my sincere thanks and gratitude to all my fellow Jamaicans for supporting me throughout the many years of my foster care experience. Without your tax participation and other forms of charitable contributions (especially throughout the time I spent at the orphanage), it would not have been possible for me to acquire life's essentials and more. Your moral and financial support is what kept me going. Besides, I am grateful that you have supported my academic dreams. So, next time when you notice your paystub reflects a little less take-home amount, it is because of someone like me who was totally dependent on someone like you. Orphan

Here is a picture of my only brother and me (from right to left, respectively). It was taken in 1979, while we were living with our former foster parents. This picture is all I have to remind me of the brother I once knew. Each time that I reflect on this picture, I can still envision my foster mother standing off to the side, signaling to us to smile. However, as you can see, smiling should be a genuine reaction that comes from the heart, not just from the lips.

children gotta eat too. I would like to remind you that when I was hungry, you gave me food; when I was thirsty, you gave me a drink; and when I was homeless, you provided a home for me. Therefore, I can say with much sincerity, that your kindness and outstanding support have not and will not be forgotten.

CHAPTER 1

THE ELUSIVENESS OF A SUPERFICIAL APPEARANCE

The Prodigious Illusion

Before I commence sharing my foster care experiences, I would like to present you with an overview of two families and ask, based on the evidence presented, which of the two you think would be the most suitable to foster a child.

The first family consisted of a middle-aged married couple who lived in a fully furnished, elegant home with their two adopted children. The wife was an assistant vice principal, and the husband had a prominent position at the Kaiser Bauxite mining company. They owned a large farm that consisted of livestock, including chickens, pigs, goats, and more. In addition to their full-time jobs and the farm, they also provided room and board for other children, which generated additional income. For the most part, they owned two motor vehicles, a minivan and a car. They both professed Christianity and assumed prominent roles (choir leader and pastoral roles) in the church they attended.

The second person was an elderly woman, two months shy of her seventieth birthday, unmarried, and with no children of her own. She resided in a little farming community, whose standard of living would be considered at or below the poverty level when compared to that of developed nations. She lived in a modest home that paled in comparison to the dwelling of the family outlined above. She did not own a motor vehicle. Her education level was equivalent to that of the sixth grade. She had no real source of income; neither did she collect any form of retirement benefits. She had a small farm (more like a home garden) and, as for livestock, had one pig, joint ownership of one cow, and a coop with less than a dozen chickens. She too professed Christianity and attended church regularly.

Based on the outline provided, which of the two families would be more suitable to foster a child? Although I am tempted to provide you with the answer, I am quite confident that it will become apparent as you continue to read my autobiography. However, here are two guiding principles that are important for us to remember. First, outward appearances can be quite deceiving. And second, generosity should not be measured by how much we have and how much we can give, but instead by what means we acquire our possessions and the genuineness by which we give. With that said, I will now transition to my first foster care experience.

The Never-ending Upheaval

My third trip away from the orphanage was much different from the previous two. This time, my brother and I were not being transferred to any of our biological parents. Instead, we were being transferred to our foster parents, whom we had never seen or heard from before. Other than the wonderful things that had been communicated to us by a representative from the CDA, we had no real concept of who our prospective foster parents really were. I distinctly remember one of the CDA representatives told us that the agency was in the process of transferring us to a foster home where we would be loved and cared for by our prospective foster parents. However, as it relates to the above premise, time will tell if "actions speak louder than words." With everything in place, we were now on our way to be united with our foster parents for the very first time.

We traveled for a while until we arrived at the CDA office that is located in Falmouth, Trelawny. Upon arrival, the CDA officer took us into the building and introduced us to our foster parents. Seeing that this was our first time meeting our foster parents, I am not sure what our reactions were. Most likely, we responded with a quick hi or hello. Moreover, the female shoes I was wearing were killing my feet! What I was most certain about was the fact that my brother and I were getting ready to add yet another dimension to our lives.

Although we had gone through many dramatic life transformations before, this one was much different, because our lives were about to take on a whole new meaning. Based on what the CDA officer had told us concerning our foster parents, I was convinced that this life-changing event would constitute the end of our lives' drama. With that in mind, I believe we can all conclude that my brother and I were getting ready to experience a "No problem man, everyting irie man" Jamaican life.

....

3

After the filing process was completed, the CDA officer waved goodbye as my brother and I departed with our foster parents. As soon as we were seated in the minivan, our foster parents commenced the journey home. Once again, it was a Toyota-made vehicle, and yes, this time, we were "moving forward" and "going places." For sure, it was nothing like that weird up-and-down, uncomfortable ride I had during my first Toyota encounter. Not only that, but this time, I had many reasons to say, "I love what you do for me, Toyota!" Okay, I should get back to my "home sweet home" episode, because I am having a little too much fun with the Toyota advertisements.

There I was, looking out the window of the minivan as we exited the town and continued on our way deep into the rural area. I was filled with endless joy and simply could not wait to arrive at my new home. By the expression on my brother's face, I knew he felt the same too. Just the mere fact that our foster parents owned a vehicle was a clear indication in my mind that this was definitely going to be a better life experience for us. But I must admit that, irrespective of the overwhelming joy I was experiencing, I was still a bit worried because I was not sure if this would turn out to be just another upheaval in our lives.

After a long ride along the winding country road, we finally pulled into the driveway of an elegant house. It had a garden that was filled with a wide variety of beautiful flowers. The scenery reminded me of a tropical paradise. Although I was a child of very few words and was unable to comprehend fully what was really happening, my first impression convinced me that this would be a better life for my brother and me. No longer would we have to go hungry, sleep out of abandoned or broken-down houses, camp out in farm huts, live on the mountain like wild animals, be shuttled back and forth to an orphanage, or be subjected to our father's Rastafarian doctrine. Knowing that those days were finally behind us was certainly a delightful feeling. Once again, the expression radiating from my brother's face was a true reflection of the joy and happiness he was experiencing as well. In comparison to the lives we had been living, this was like marching out of the wilderness into the promised land.

My thought process was interrupted when my foster mother opened the door and beckoned to us to come out of the vehicle. We did accordingly, and she escorted us inside the house. The minute I stepped inside the house, I was overwhelmed with even more joy because I simply could not believe that I would be living in such a beautiful home. Never before had I seen a home display so much beauty and elegance! It was breathtaking! (However, it did not take long for my brother and me to find out that beauty was only the tangible thing that we could see, not the hearts and minds of those who possessed it. This revelation will become apparent shortly.) Just as the pixie dust was about to carry me away to the land of utopia, my foster mother interrupted my awe moment with an important introduction. She introduced us to three other children, Michael, Joy, and Barry. They did not run and embrace us, but instead said hi from a distance. They were looking a bit curious, as if they were not expecting us. Or it could be that they were surprised to see a boy wearing a pair of female shoes. Now that I think about it, I would most likely have had the same reaction. Well, stick around because there is plenty of female-shoe drama to come.

At the time, I did not have any concept of age but, in hindsight, it was obvious that Joy and Barry appeared to be in their early teens, while Michael appeared to be somewhere around six or seven years old. So who were these children? Joy and Michael were our foster parents' adopted children, while Barry was my foster mother's nephew. The more pressing question, however, is who in their right minds would go out of their way to foster two additional children when they already had three to contend with?

As you continue to read my autobiography, you will discover that my foster parents established a clear distinction as it related to their actions toward the adopted and fostered children. For example, the first distinct difference was the fact that the two adopted children's surnames were changed to that of my foster parents while the foster children were not. The next difference was in the manner in which we were told to address our foster parents, more so our foster mother. We, the foster children, were forbidden from addressing our foster mother as mom, mummy, or any other label that would imply that we had established an emotional bond that she deemed too personal. I would like to point out that throughout the initial stage, we were allowed to address our foster mother as mummy. However, after about the third month she told us not to address her in such a manner. I will discuss this and the other subtle differences later.

My foster parents welcomed the foster children into their home with the sole intention of providing them with the essentials, such as food, clothes, shelter, and basic education, in exchange for how much financial gain and manual labor that they could extract from the CDA and the foster children. As harsh as it may seem, from my foster parents' perspective, intangibles such as love and affection were considered not part of the deal. My foster parents treated the foster children as though they (foster parents) had a contractual agreement (between them and the CDA), which they could terminate at any time for any reason. When the foster children were no longer of any economic value to them, they were returned to the CDA or, as it was in my brother's case, transferred to a juvenile correctional institution.

Now that you have had a very brief overview of the differences between the children who were fostered and the children who were adopted, I will proceed by outlining the first day's experience with my foster parents. After my brother and I were introduced to the other three children, we were given a tour of the house. Once again, this was the biggest and most elegant home I had ever seen! It had four fully furnished bedrooms, three bathrooms, spacious living and dining rooms, a kitchen, a laundry room, two verandahs, and a garage. The living room had several exquisite couches (settees, as per Jamaicans) and a very large flat-screen television. Okay, please forget the "flat screen" description because no such television was around in 1978, but you get the point. Regardless, it was a rather large television. The kitchen was equipped with a gas stove (another gas stove and an electric two-burner hot plate stove were added later) for cooking. Nothing like the wood fire that I was accustomed to while living with my parents. Later I found out that the house was also equipped with other household amenities such as washing machines, electric floor polishers, and electric clothes irons. In addition, my foster parents had a helper (more

like a servant from their perspective) who was responsible for cleaning, washing, and assisting with the prepara-
tion of meals and other household chores. From a Third
World perspective, my foster parents' standard of living
was comparable to that of the average American middle-
class family. My foster parents' house had all the tangible
things a house needed to bring about the desired comfort
but, unfortunately, it lacked the two most essentials, love
and compassion. In other words, it had everything that
was needed for it to be classified as a house, but none of
what was required for it to be considered a home.

Anyway, for the moment everything was going great!
I was overwhelmed with joy to the point that I had totally
forgotten that I was wearing a pair of female shoes. I was
not sure if any of my foster parent's children had noticed
that I was wearing a pair of visible, white, high-heeled
shoes. It could have been that they had but were simply
waiting for the right moment to direct a few laughs my
way. Regardless of the situation, I was spared for the
moment. At the end of the grand tour, our foster mother
provided us with clean clothes and told us to take showers
and get dressed.[3] After we were through showering and
dressed in our finest attire, our foster mother told us to go
and have a seat at the elegant dining table. I found out
later that taking a shower before sitting around the dining
table was one of our foster mother's most sacred rules. Let
me rephrase, my brother and I dared not take a seat any-

---

3 In retrospect, I am beginning to wonder why my brother and I were always
summoned to go shower the minute we arrived at the orphanage and now at
our foster parents' home. It appeared as though the orphanage and our foster
parents did not trust our squeaky-clean appearance. Okay, I must admit that
every time we showed up at the orphanage, we were always in need of showers.

where in the dining room unless we had showered first. Notice that I did not mention the living room, because the couches were completely off limits for us.

After dinner was served, the entire family, except for Barry, sat at our designated areas around the elegant dining table. At the time, I had no idea why Barry was not allowed to join the rest of the family at the dining table. Probably he did not maintain proper hygiene because he was caring for the farm animals and chickens. Or could it be that he did not display the royal-like etiquette deemed necessary by my foster mother? I may never know because I did not inquire of Barry the reason why he did not join the family at the dining table.

Anyway, my first meal experience turned out to be quite a spectacle when I attempted to eat with the aid of a knife and a fork. At first, I felt as though I was a member of the royal family. However, I soon realized that this was simply too much elegance for me because that afternoon most of my dinner, including my dumpling, ended up on the floor. I must admit that none of this would have happened had it not been for those rubbery Jamaican flour dumplings. Jamaican dumplings are so rubbery they could be used as a substitute for Goodyear and Bridgestone motor tires. Although my description of the dumplings was a bit over the top, I can assure you that the rubbery effect of the dumpling was the cause of my problem.

After witnessing my first dining-room drama, my foster mother realized that this elegance was simply too much for me. With that said, she instructed Joy to cut my dumpling into smaller pieces. Not only that, but from that day forward, I was never allowed to use a knife again. My brother was able to use his utensils, but that was short-lived because, according to our foster mother, we displayed poor table etiquette (more on this incident shortly). After we were through with dinner, we watched television for a while. At approximately 7:30 p.m., we ate a light snack. Finally, at approximately 9:00 p.m., we retired to bed. I must emphasize that, at the time, I had limited or no knowledge of the fundamentals of life concerning numbers, letters of the alphabet, distance, time of day, days, weeks, months, years, and many of the other vital developmental skills a child my age should have had. Therefore, my references in such regard are based on my experience and knowledge in retrospect.

Here is a breakdown of the living accommodations: Barry, George, and I occupied one of the four rooms. Barry slept on a king-sized bed, while my brother and I shared a twin bed. Michael and Joy shared another room located on the opposite side of the house, adjacent to our foster parents' room. The fourth room was vacant because my foster parents used it to board children who were attending high schools that were within proximity. In the initial stage, everything was going great! Or, as we say in Jamaica, "Everyting irie man!" Not even the dumpling drama or the female shoes could put a damper on the joy that was radiating deep within my soul. However, despite the optimistic outlook, I would like for you to please remain seated with your seatbelts fastened because there is much turbulence ahead.

The Dawn of a New Day

The following morning, I woke up to the melodious barking, chirping, quacking, and crowing sounds that were reverberating throughout the backyard. Later that morning, the rest of the family, including my brother, got up. I could hear the bangarang (noise) coming from the kitchen, which was a clear indication someone was preparing breakfast. We were instructed by Barry to go to the bathroom and wash our faces and brush our teeth. Brushing of teeth was new for my brother and me because at the orphanage the children would eat the toothpaste instead of using it to brush their teeth. I mean, an entire tube of toothpaste would be consumed in less than an hour. I guess we were more concerned with having clean digestive tracts rather than sporting pearly white teeth. No need to talk about the time we spent with our mother, because we did not even have so much as a toothbrush. However, while living with our father, we used Chew sticks (sometimes advertised as Chewsticks or Chewing Sticks) to brush our teeth.

After completing our required hygiene ritual, Barry, Michael, George, and I sat in the room and engaged in sporadic conversation until breakfast was served. After breakfast was served, we, except for Barry, sat around the elegant dining table. I am not too keen on the specifics, however, from what I can recall, breakfast was most likely the regular Saturday morning: scrambled eggs with sausage, hard dough bread, and a cup of hot Milo (chocolate) beverage. In Jamaica, we suffix all hot beverages with the word tea. Therefore, in this case, we simply say, "Milo tea." At first, I had no idea what day of the week it was, however, later I found out that it was a Saturday based on the day's activities; and more accurately, the information that is recorded in my file.

After we were through with our breakfasts, everyone got very busy with the farm and household chores. Joy assisted with the light in-house duties, which included preparing and sorting the clothes and bed linens for the week's laundry. She also replaced the flowers in the vases with fresh ones from the garden. The helper was tasked with the laundry and the cleaning duties. My brother and I were asked to assist Barry with the farm chores. First, we started out by cleaning the chicken and rabbit coops. Second, we placed fresh wood dust on the floors of the chicken coops. Third, we washed and restocked the feeding containers with feed and water. Fourth, we harvested fresh grass from the property across the street and used it as feed for the rabbits. Fifth, and final, my brother and I assisted Michael with the yard chores, which included sweeping and raking the excess leaves and loose soil from the paved and open areas of the yard. Before I proceed, I would like to point out that neither my brother nor I were given any protective attire such as shoes or gloves while working on the farm. Therefore, we had to carry out the farm chores barefooted. As for Barry, he was fortunate to have an old pair of our foster father's work boots.

My foster mother coordinated the activities to ensure that they were completed satisfactorily. That is, she made sure that the animals' and birds' enclosures were cleaned and that they were fed promptly; the laundry was done satisfactorily; the floor and the furniture were spotless (displayed a mirror-like effect); and that the yard was swept squeaky clean.

Our foster father was not with us that morning because he was still at the Kaiser Bauxite mining company where he worked a full-time job. On that particular week, he worked the graveyard/midnight shift. He came home approximately 9:00 a.m., ate his breakfast, and then sat on the front verandah and read the newspaper. After reading the paper (probably looking for coupons; not really), he ran a couple of errands. That day we watched an episode of the most popular "Ring Ding" children's program presented by Lou Bennett-Coverley, otherwise known as Miss Lou.

At noon when we were through with our chores, we ate lunch and talked for a while. Lunch consisted of a glass of lemonade and two slices of hard dough bread with a spread of butter. My brother and I were told not to sit at the dining table for lunch. Most likely this was the case because we had not yet showered and dressed in clean attire. In fact, we were not allowed to congregate inside the house unless we had taken a shower and dressed in clean clothes. With that said, we sat with Barry on the little wooden bench located on the back verandah.

Later that afternoon, my foster mother prepared dinner. If my memory is correct, I believe it was a large pot of chicken soup. However, just before dinner was served, my brother and I assisted Barry with the farm chores as we had earlier that morning. Our foster parents did raise quite a lot of chickens, rabbits, and guinea pigs. As time progressed, pigs, goats, cows, and bees were added to the farm. By that time, however, Barry was no longer living with the family, which meant that my brother and I had to assume full responsibility for all the farm chores.

On average, Fridays and Saturdays were reserved for slaughtering animals and chickens. Although we did not slaughter any chickens that day, shortly after that, this practice became one of the more labor-intensive weekend activities. On a typical weekend, we spent an average of twelve hours (7:00 a.m. to 7:00 p.m.) slaughtering, plucking, and bagging chickens to be sold to the locals. At the end of the day, my hands were wrinkled to the point that it appeared as though I were 1000 years old.

My brother and I were not allowed to attend school most Fridays and occasionally one or two other weekdays because we were tasked with assisting the butchers. We were responsible for gathering the firewood that the butchers used to heat large containers of water. The hot water was used to remove the hair and the feathers from the slaughtered pigs and chickens, respectively. We also had to clean the animals' (goats and pigs) head, feet, and organs (tripe). As I was writing this segment, I could not help but wonder what my father would have done had he found out that my brother and I were participating in the Babylonian activities that he utterly despised.

Nonetheless, before I delved too deep into what is to come, let me get back to the first day's activities. So, after we were through with the farm chores, we showered, dressed in clean clothes, walked gingerly to the table, and sat at our designated areas. My foster mother implemented the strictest table etiquette one could ever imagine. I can assure you that this was much different from what we were accustomed to while living at the orphanage. We had better not let the fork or spoon make contact with our teeth. If we did, our foster mother would get our attention by tapping on the table, followed by one of her frightening, eye-popping stares. Her most notable comment was, "Stop chopping your mouth like pigs!" Besides, we could not make any slurping sounds with our mouths while eating or drinking. We had to chew our food and drink our soups and beverages quietly and methodically. So one could only imagine how mealtime would turn out to be a daunting task for us.

Later that evening, we watched an episode of "Little House on the Prairie" while enjoying a scoop of ice cream and a slice of fruitcake. However, the "good times" lasted for a couple of weeks for my brother and me. As the old saying goes, "Enjoy it while it lasts." After we were through with our snacks, we were summoned to bed. And that pretty much concluded that first full day of life with our foster parents.

The following day (Sunday), everyone was up bright and early. Once again, I was awakened by the noise that was echoing from the farm animals and birds. Before starting the day's chores, we were all summoned to the dining room for the morning's devotion. After everyone was seated at the dining table, we commenced the morning's devotion by singing songs (no reggae, only gospel), followed by the reading of scripture verses. Everyone except George and I took turns reading a verse or two from the Bible. I remember when it was our turn to read, we did not have a clue what was written in the Bible. I mean, we did not know the first word, the second word, the third . . . With that said, the decision was made to exclude us from the reading. Even Michael (our foster mother's adopted son), who was only in the first grade was able to read fluently. Instead of picking up the Bible and glossing over the words as if we were great academic scholars from Princeton, Harvard, or the University of the West Indies, my brother and I should have immediately taken a pass when it was our turn to read. After the reading, my foster father prompted a short discussion through open dialogue. Once again, my brother and I remained quiet because we had little or no clue what was being discussed. Finally, the morning's devotion was concluded with a closing prayer.

Hope Gospel Hall Church

This Sunday morning ritual lasted only for a short while because it was eventually phased out. I am not sure why.

After the devotion, Barry, my brother, and I completed the morning chores just as we had the previous day. However, one additional chore that was unique to Sundays was the detail cleaning of the minivan. I mean, it had to be cleaned from top to bottom, inside, and outside. The minivan was used to transport the family and several other church members to and from the church. After all the chores were completed, we showered, ate breakfast, and got dressed for church.

Do you remember the pair of girl's shoes that I wore from the orphanage? The ones I thought I would be wearing only once because my foster parents would immediately replace them with a pair of male shoes. Well, I hope you have not forgotten because a series of unforgettable shoe dramas is about to unfold in what I would like to classify as "The Inner Soles."

After I was through eating breakfast, I got dressed but was a bit hesitant to put on the pair of female shoes. I was hoping that my foster mother would provide me with a pair of male shoes. However, to my surprise and dismay, what I had been hoping for did not happen. Instead, my foster mother told me that she did not have a pair of shoes for me and that I should wear the pair I had. Right then and there, I knew that I was about to become everyone's laughingstock. Not wanting to spoil the good relationship I had experienced thus far, I went ahead and put on the pair of girl's shoes.

The very minute I stepped out of the room, I could see my own family members trying desperately to hold back the laughter. Remember, I had not yet gone beyond the comfort of the home, and things had already taken an ugly turn. Can you imagine the barrage of insults that is about to be levied at me by the children when I arrived at church?

Nonetheless, it was time to leave, so we went into the minivan and made ourselves comfortable while waiting for our parents. Shortly after that, our parents came in, and we commenced our journey to the church, which was located approximately six and a half miles away from home. As we drove through the little farming districts, we picked up several church members along the way. After a ride of approximately twenty to thirty minutes, we finally reached our destination at the Hope Gospel Hall church located in Sawyers, Trelawny.

After the people who were ahead of me got off, I made a mad dash out of the vehicle and into the building, hoping not to be noticed by anyone, especially the children. However, the minute I stepped into the building, a number of the children started laughing at me. Even a few of the adults snickered too. It's true! I could see the expressions on their faces. Nonetheless, I went and sat on one of the benches and sort of tucked my feet far underneath the bench in front of me. That did not stop the other children from noticing that I was wearing a pair of white female shoes. I could hear the children behind me whispering, "Bwoy, a weh yuh a duh in a de gal shoes?" ("Boy, what are you doing wearing a pair of girl shoes?") I sat there hoping that the church ceremony would be over as quickly as possible but, instead, it dragged on as though it would never end. What a way to begin the day!

Finally, the eternal church service ended! The children and the adults got up and started walking around and conversing with each other. The subject was mostly about my brother and me, seeing that this was our first time attending the church. I remained seated because I did not want to endure further humiliation. After sitting there for a while, my foster parents bid goodbye to the other church members and signaled to us that it was time to go. I got up and ran into the vehicle to avoid being laughed at again. Even while I was sitting in the vehicle, a number of the annoying children came by the window and taunted me some more. They were saying things like, "Bwoy! Mi she, gu home tek aff de gal shoes." ("Boy! I said, go home and take off the girl shoes!") I can assure you that it was a relief for me when my foster father came into the vehicle, and we commenced our journey home.

The minute we arrived home, I was the very first one out of the vehicle. As soon as my foster mother opened the door, I ran inside and removed the pair of girl's shoes from my feet as quickly as I could. That certainly provided me with a wonderful relief from the mental and physical pain that was radiating throughout my soles. Let me emphasize that it was absolutely no fun walking around in a pair of high-heeled girl's shoes. (Well, to be factual, the pair of shoes that I was wearing had more like semi-high heels and not high heels like those worn by many fashion models.)

The usual Sunday afternoon routine started out with my foster mother and her adopted daughter, Joy, finalizing the dinner preparations that they had started earlier that morning. While dinner was being prepared, George, Barry, Michael, and I sat in the backyard and indulged in a casual afternoon conversation. When dinner was served, we all sat around the elegant (at least from my perspective) dining table, except for Barry, who once again sat on the little wooden bench on the back verandah.

For those who are not familiar with the Jamaican culture, here is a little Sunday Culture 101. Jamaicans take great pride in their Sunday meals. I always looked forward to a delicious Sunday dinner when possible. Notice I used the words "when possible." In fact, enjoying a delicious Sunday meal was not financially feasible while I was living with my mother. Although my father had the financial means, Sunday's meal was no different from any other day's meal. In fact, it was mostly ital soup. Moreover, preparing and serving meat was in stark contrast to his Rastafarian doctrine. I must emphasize that we had received delicious Sunday meals while living at the orphanage, but my foster parents' meals were a lot more elegant. In general, our Sunday meals were the traditional

Jamaican dishes, including rice and beans, baked, fried or brown stewed chicken, and vegetables. For the beverage, we were served a tall glass of carrot, papaya, soursop, or some other homemade fruit or vegetable juice. Okay, no need to elaborate further because the point has been established that Jamaican Sunday meals are considered special. Throughout the week (except Saturday, which is a soup day), we were served steamed callaloo or cabbage with brown stewed chicken, curried chicken, stewed beef, curried goat, or canned corned beef.

After dinner, Michael, George, and I removed the dirty dishes and utensils from the table. After we were through clearing the dining room, my brother and I washed the dishes and scoured the pots and pans. Finally, we mopped the kitchen floor. Later that afternoon, we assisted Barry with the feeding of the animals and the chickens. While we were busy with our chores, our foster parents sat on the verandah and had their grown-up conversation. Most likely, their conversation was about my brother and me and the extreme effort that would be required to bring our academic standing up to the kindergarten level. Okay, let me not speculate because I did not have a clue of what their conversation was about, but if it was not about us, then what else could have caused them to convene such an urgent summit? Anyway, after all the chores were completed, Barry, George, and I sat in the backyard and engaged in another chitchat rapport.

Later that evening, we were summoned by our foster mother to get ready for the Sunday evening church service. Everyone was dressed in appropriate attire except for me. I had no other choice but to wear a pair of female shoes. Once again, we commenced our journey to the

Hope Gospel Hall. Just like earlier, we picked up a number of church members along the way. However, it was déjà vu all over again because the minute I stepped out of the vehicle, the children started mocking me as if they had not gotten enough entertainment that morning. I ran into the building, sat on one of the benches, and remained seated for the duration of service. I mean, I did not even get up to go to the restroom. However, that did not deter the children because the ones who were sitting behind me continued mocking me throughout the service, as if that was the sole reason why they had come to church. Once again, I became the laughingstock for the children.

After the night service ended, we went home. As soon as the vehicle pulled into the driveway and my foster mother opened the house door, I ran inside and, once again, ripped the pair of shoes off my feet as quickly as possible. It was a physical and psychological relief not to have that pair of female shoes on my feet. Shortly after that, the family gathered in the dining room, and we enjoyed a light snack. The family, except my brother and I, conversed for a short while, then we all retired to bed.

Instead of taking you through each day's routine, I will instead fast-forward to the next major set of events that is worth sharing. I knew that Christmas was fast approaching because Christmas carols were being played on the radio and the church members were rehearsing for the upcoming Christmas program. I was designated to be the little drummer boy for the "Come, they told me, pa rum pum pum" song. After having gone through many countless hours of rehearsals, on the day of the program, I refused to go on the stage and play the drum. I was simply too embarrassed to be seen on stage in front of a large congregation wearing a pair of female shoes. I remember the program coordinator announced my name and the part I was designated to play several times. However, instead of getting up out of my seat and walking bravely onto the stage with my little bongo drum, I decided to sit in my seat and remain quiet as though I did not know what was going on. When the program coordinator was unable to persuade me, my foster mother intervened. She came over to where I was sitting and stared at me with her eyes bulging out of her head like a total lunar eclipse. Oh boy, this outcome became a terrifying experience for me. Anyway, despite my refusal to participate, the Christmas program went on because Barry had to take over the drummer boy role. Notwithstanding "The Little Drummer Boy" mishap, the Christmas festive season was an enjoyable one.

The holiday finally ended when my brother and I were given uniforms and told that the following day we would be attending school. Although I was excited, I was a bit nervous because of my past experience at Anchovy Primary School. That night, my brother and I were given two whole notebooks (English and math subjects, respectively) and one whole pencil each. Let me repeat. My brother and I were given two notebooks and one whole pencil each! Nothing like the half of a notebook and the one-third of a pencil we had received while residing at the orphanage. Well, I should not be such a downer on the orphanage because while living with my father attending school had been forbidden. And from my mother's perspective, education was not important. In fact, while living with my father, my siblings and I attended school for approximately four to six weeks, and throughout that time, we were never given any school supplies. While living with my mother, my brother and I did not attend school, not even for a single day. With that in mind, I should not have any qualms with the orphanage for enacting their stringent resource-sharing policy.

Who Are These Girls, and Why Are They Here?

That Sunday afternoon, out of the blue, two teenaged girls somewhat magically appeared into the family. Hmmm, I wonder what orphanage they came from? Okay, they were not from an orphanage, but instead, they were boarding with the family because it was not practical for them to commute to and from their respective homes and assigned school. They were attending the Westwood (girls' only) High school, located in Stewart Town, Trelawney. This school was approximately two miles from my foster parents' home. I also found out that they were already boarding with my foster parents, but had gone home to be with their families for the Christmas holiday. Including these two girls, there were now seven children living at home. Other than their names (Hillary and Judith) and the fact that they were boarding with my foster parents, I did not know them that well because my brother and I viewed them as being privileged rather than our peers. By the way, we had the same view concerning our foster parents' adopted children. This class structure was not something that was written or established with spoken words but, instead, it was subtle innuendos that guided our behavior.

The Anticipated Drama

That Sunday night, we were summoned to bed much earlier than usual. I was very much excited but at the same time quite nervous about how I would fit in at school. Before I knew it, it was Monday morning, the first day of school. I remember getting up very early, but my foster mother and Joy were already in the kitchen preparing breakfast. Joy and the boarders left quite early because they attended Westwood High School, which commenced earlier than the all-age and the primary schools. Shortly after that, the rest of the family, except my foster father, woke up and commenced the morning chores. My foster mother prepared breakfast while Barry assumed full responsibility for the farm chores.

For the first couple of days, George and I were not assigned any morning chores. However, that changed rather quickly when we were told to get up much earlier and buff the floors throughout the house. Not only that, but within a couple of weeks, we were assigned full responsibility to take care of the farm animals and birds because Barry was removed from the home. I will put this in perspective shortly.

Barry was the only child who was not attending school. He was not allowed to pursue his education beyond the ninth grade. Instead, he worked at a small home-based candy shop while tending to my foster parents' farm.

So what was our first school experience like? As for our uniforms, I would like to say that they were a bit supersized. My foster mother was very cost-conscious as it related to foster children. The first visible indication was the fact that she made poor choices regarding our attire.

Whenever she went shopping, she would deliberately purchase clothes and footwear that were two or three sizes larger than our actual sizes. Most likely, she intended for them to last two or three times longer. Sneakers were the most obvious, not to mention our shirts. She made our shirts herself, and they were so big that it appeared as though we were dressed in Superman's cape. Okay, I should not get too carried away with the shirts because that turned out to be the least of my problems.

I was hoping and praying that I would not have to wear the pair of female shoes to school, but unfortunately, that was not the case because my foster mother did not buy me a pair of sneakers. If you think that wearing a pair of female shoes to church was humiliating, embarrassing, and downright depressing, then just wait until you hear what happened to me while I was at school, where there were hundreds of pesky children to contend with. That morning I remember putting on my khaki uniform but I refused to put on the pair of female shoes. I was hoping that my foster mother would surprise me with a pair of sneakers but, once again, I was only dreaming. By the way, in Jamaica, sneakers are also referred to as crepe. Anyway, the minute my foster mother looked at my feet and noticed that I did not have on any shoes, in a commanding tone she said, "Guh put on yuh shoes. Wi ready fi leave!" ("Go and put on your shoes! We are ready to leave!") Right then and there I knew that she had not bought me a pair of sneakers. Despite my reservations, I went ahead and put on the pair of female shoes. I must admit that I was a bit jealous of Michael because he was fully dressed in his brand new, well fitted, readymade uniform and sneakers. He was not wearing any homemade

Stewart Town All-Age School, today it is known as Stewart Town Primary.

My 2nd grade classroom

uniform and certainly not wearing a pair of female shoes either.

I realized my first rude awakening when I had to walk approximately three hundred yards on an unpaved road to the bus stop. Let me emphasize that walking on an unpaved road in female, semi-high-heeled shoes was undoubtedly a test of my Achilles' heels! I believe that all women who wear high heels are gluttons for severe punishment. It is mind-boggling to fathom a person wearing heels that are two or three times taller than the ones I wore and still being able to maintain her balance. Much kudos to you fashion models out there.

Anyway, back to my ordeal. Finally we arrived at the bus stop! After a wait of ten to fifteen minutes, a mini commuter bus arrived and we went on board with much haste. Or as we say in Jamaica, "Hurry up, man!" The minibus drove for a while, picking up and letting off passengers along the way. There were many students on the bus but, lucky for me, none of them had noticed that I was wearing a pair of female shoes. Or could it have been that they were waiting until my foster mother was not around before they start mocking me? Once again, I tucked my feet underneath the seat in front of me, hoping that no one would notice.

After several stops, the minibus finally made it to Stewart Town. Stewart Town is a little farming district that is located in the parish of Trelawny. After the minibus came to a stop, the teachers and students, including my foster mother, Michael, George, and I got off the bus. Just when I thought my walk was over, I found out that it had only just begun. I had to walk another quarter of a mile from the bus depot to where the school was located.

I started out walking briskly, keeping pace with the crowd. My whole concern was to disguise my feet so that no one would notice that I was wearing a pair of female shoes. And luckily for me, no one had noticed. At least that was what I thought. After the long and gruesome walk, I finally arrived at the Stewart Town All-Age School.

Everything was going according to plan. Or, as we say in Jamaica, "No problem man, everyting irie!" Oops, forget what I have just said regarding concealing my feet because, in the words of Apollo 13, "Houston, we've had a problem." As soon as I stepped through the school gate, a number of the boys noticed that I was wearing a pair of girl's shoes. Immediately they burst out laughing and said, "Bwoy! A wah dat yuh hab pan yuh foot, bwoy?" ("Boy! What is that you have on your feet, boy?") Within a couple of seconds, all the children who were present started laughing and mocking me. I was so humiliated. I really wanted to go back home or just disappear. However, none of that happened. Instead, I had to stand there and face the wrath of my fellow schoolmates. Finally, the bell rang, which gave me temporary relief. The ringing of the bell signaled the children that it was time to prepare for the morning's devotion.

The children formed three queues, which represented the different houses or teams. The houses were Laing, March, and Sievwright. I might be off with the spellings but consider it to be 99.99 percent accurate. My brother and I were assigned to the March and Laing houses, respectively. After a headcount, we were allowed to proceed to the devotion hall. When all the children were gathered in the open hall, one of the teachers commenced the devotion period with the singing of songs followed by the reading of several scripture verses from the Bible. Once again, there is no real separation of church and state like in the United States of America. After we were through with the singing and reading, the principal, Mr. Nelson, welcomed the students and teachers back to school and outlined the agenda for the rest of the school year.

After we were through with the devotion, the students dispersed to their various classes, except for a small number of new students, which included my brother and me. We had not yet been assigned to any class. Shortly after that, George and I were assigned to the third and second grade, respectively. And would you believe that I was jeered and mocked while I was being accompanied by my teacher, Mrs. Palmer, to my assigned classroom. I just could not catch a break!

However, my brother and I had a much bigger problem, which had more to do with our academic standing. Concerning literacy, we were at a severe disadvantage when compared with our peers. Don't believe me? Then here is a snapshot. I was unable to recite the letters of the alphabet, which includes the letters A to Z. By the way, the letter Z is pronounced zee if you are residing in the United States and zed if you are living in the UK and the Commonwealth. It did not matter if it was pronounced zee, zed, or zebra because I did not understand the significance of the alphabet. Not only that, but I could not recite the days of the week or the months of the year. I did not have a clue with regard to time, which meant that I was unable to make any inference or reference in such regard. Even if someone had placed Big Ben before my face, I would not have known what time of the day it was. And don't even put math into the equation because the circle was the only geometric figure I was able to identify. Whenever the instructor asked us to recite the time table, I had no clue what she was saying. Probably I thought she meant how many times I sat at the table. Not really, but I am quite sure you get the point that I was on a different planet as it pertained to my academic standing. My brother's academic standing was not much better than mine either. Therefore, I could rightfully conclude that instead of being placed in the second and third grade, we should have been placed at the kindergarten level. As you can see, we needed a thousand miracles just to make it through our respective grades.

The Relentless Mocking of My Soles

So let's find out how the rest of my school day transpired. After the roll call, Mrs. Palmer commenced the day's lesson. However, I had no clue what she was saying. I just sat there in a daze for the duration. Shortly after that, the bell rang to signify that it was time for our first fifteen-minute break. Silly me! I got up out of my seat and ventured outside to play with the other boys. However, I found out rather quickly that none of my classmates or schoolmates wanted to play or even to be seen socializing with me. Instead, they were saying things like, "Move fram yasso bwoy! Wi nuh ramp wid bwoy inna gal shoes." ("Move away from here boy! We do not play with a boy who wears girl shoes.") My brother looked on helplessly as I was being harassed by my fellow schoolmates.

The bell rang again to alert the children that it was time to get back to their respective classes. And guess what! The mocking and jeering did not stop. Throughout the entire class session, a few of my classmates continued to mock me as if they had not done enough already. I mean, the mocking kept coming at me from all sides. Even one or two of the girls joined in with the boys to poke fun at me. I could not concentrate. I just wanted to go home and get the darn (to put it mildly) pair of shoes off my feet! Unfortunately, that was not an option. Time was simply not on my side either, because the hours kept going by very slowly.

Later the bell rang for the third time to signify that it was lunchtime. Instead of leaving the classroom with the other students, I waited until they were all gone. As soon as I was the only one left inside the classroom, I got up and ran quickly to my foster mother's classroom, which was next door. One would think that having lunch with my foster mother would have allowed me a break from those pesky children. If that's what you are thinking, then you are most certainly wrong. In fact, a number of the boys would come by the classroom and whisper under their breath, "Bwoy, mi seh gu tekaff de gal shoes." ("Boy, I said go and take off the girl shoes.") It appeared as though they had sacrificed their lunch hour just to come by and mock me some more. Even my foster mother chuckled and said, "You boys are troublemakers." I was too embarrassed to go out into the schoolyard. So, after lunch, I sat in my foster mother's classroom and stayed there for the remainder of the lunch break. I had no other choice but to sit there and watch while the other children were outside playing and having fun.

After the lunch period was over, the bell rang again, and the children dispersed to their respective classes. After the children were settled in, the teacher continued with the day's lesson until she was interrupted by the bell, which signified that it was time for our afternoon break. I did not leave the classroom because I knew that the other children were camped out in the schoolyard like vicious predators just waiting for me to venture out onto the open plains. Having learned my lesson earlier that day, I decided to stay in the classroom. Finally, the evening bell rang, and we, or should I say, the other children recited the scary Halloween-like going-home song. Let me see if I remember some of it. "Now the day is over, night is drawing nigh. Shadows of the evening steal across the sky." Very scary, isn't it? However, I should not be afraid of the evening ritual; instead, I should be more fearful of those annoying children! So once again, I waited until all the children had left the classroom before I ventured out of my seat.

After they were gone out of sight (but not out of mind), I made a mad dash to my foster mother's classroom. However, the ordeal was not yet over. I was picked on while walking with my foster mother to the bus stop. A number of the boys would sneak up behind me and whisper, while others would run by and shout at me. They were all conveying the same message: "Bwoy, mi seh guh tekaff de gal shoes." ("Boy, I said go and take off the girl shoes.") They did that for the entire journey to the town square. After arriving at the town square, we did not have to wait too long, because within a couple of minutes a minibus arrived and we went on board and headed for home. As soon as I got home, I took the pair of shoes off my feet as quickly as possible. Oh boy! What a relief! I had made it through the first day of physical and psychological anguish. Well, I had better not get used to this temporary relief because, within a couple of hours, I would have to go through this ordeal all over again. I did not learn a single thing that day because I was too caught up with the hilarious but painful shoe drama. I would do anything not to wear the pair of girl shoes another day, but that was only wishful thinking.

Tuesday was pretty much the same as Monday. That is, the relentless mocking/jeering/taunting continued. It appeared as though the news regarding my wearing a pair of female shoes was spreading around to all the students like wildfire. Not only that, but each day I was being mocked by many more students. Everywhere I went, I was drawing a big crowd as if I were a famous celebrity or a high-ranking politician. Physically I was in school, but mentally, my mind had wandered off into a distant land.

To this very day, I still do not understand why my foster mother did not take the initiative to buy me a pair of sneakers, even though she was fully aware that every day I was being mocked and shunned by my fellow schoolmates! I can only surmise that she did not think that my psychological pain was worth the monetary cost. However, as time progressed, the persistent mocking and jeering subsided because the students had gotten used to my female shoes' drama.

Before I proceed, I would like to make a solemn plea to everyone, especially preteens and teenagers. There have been too many children who have committed suicide because they have been bullied and humiliated at school, on social media, or through other venues. I can attest to their psychological and mental anguish because I endured similar bullying throughout my childhood years. This bullying was apparent while living at the orphanage and even more so throughout the times when I was teased, shunned, and humiliated because I was forced to wear a pair of female shoes. Throughout such times, I would have done anything not to go to school or church so that I would not have to succumb to the psychological pain anymore. I have to thank God that, throughout such times, the thought of suicide never entered my mind because if it had, then there is a high probability that I may not be alive today. Here is my advice for those children who think that it is okay or funny to go around bullying others because they might look different or because they might be going through afflictions: Please ask yourself, "If I were in that person's shoes [in my case this was both metaphorical and literal] or someday find myself in an unfortunate situation, would I want to be bullied and or ridiculed by others?" Also, for the parents, please remember that in this context responsible parenting goes a long way.

Nonetheless, I should not be too concerned with the female shoes because this, as you are about to find out, was the least of my problems. Up to this point, my brother and I had been living a life of illusion as it related to the true nature of our foster parents, more so our foster mother. With that said, we were about to discover that our foster parents were the complete opposite of what the CDA representative had promised. I will now share with you several experiences that will bring you closer to understanding what life was like for the foster children (mainly my brother) who were subjected to my foster parents' inhumane treatment.

PARENTING PHILOSOPHIES

All Good Things Have Come to an End

Here is the incident that gave us our first rude awakening concerning the type of people our foster parents really were. One evening (most likely on the third or fourth day of school), after my brother and I were through with our chores, our foster mother summoned us to go and complete our school assignments. As for me, I was simply too distracted by the whole shoe drama, which meant that I had very little knowledge of what was going on at school. Actually, I should not be blaming the shoes or the mocking and jeering because regardless of the distraction, the outcome would have been the same. That is, I was indeed an illiterate child who did not belong in the second grade. However, it did not take long for my foster mother to notice that I was not doing any homework, which prompted her to ask me to write my name. I did not have a clue to the significance of the letters of the alphabet, much less to figure out the combination of letters that constitute the spelling of my name. Oh boy! I found myself in a very embarrassing situation! There I was six months shy of my eleventh birthday, having been assigned to the second grade, and still with no clue how to even spell my name!

As soon as my foster mother discovered that I was unable to spell my name, I remember she made a couple of big laughs, followed by a "Lawd Jeezas!" ("Lord Jesus!") outburst. Her laughter was not one of concern, but one of discontent. Immediately after that, she raised her voice and said, "The big bwoy in a de second grade and can't even spell im name!" ("The big boy is in the second grade and is unable to spell his name.") George was summoned to do the same, and found himself in the same predicament. I am not sure how my brother had managed to disguise his illiteracy from our foster mother for the first couple of school days. With such a revelation, our little secret of not being able to read or write was now out in the open and, from that point forward, we paid dearly. We were struck many times on our fingers with a ruler, beaten with leather straps garden hose, and sticks, pinched, slapped, knocked on our heads, had our ears pinched and tugged on, and made to stand in all sorts of stress-inducing positions until we were able to meet the basic academic requirements.

What should have been a typical teaching and learning session was always a very fearful and painful experience for us. I was unable to learn much because of her constant yelling and the intense pain caused by her many forms of physical punishment; thus making it impossible for me to understand her commands. Our learning process was slow, and it was painful. Many nights after enduring all sorts of punishment, we were relieved when our foster mother gave up on us and told us to go to bed. Even to this very day, reading out loud is still a fearful experience for me. Our foster mother did not even stop to think that she had just rescued us from an orphanage and not from a home where we had been given opportunities and all the resources in the world to learn but had refused to do so! My foster mother's reaction caused me to wonder if the CDA representative had not informed her regarding our academic standing.

Isn't it ironic that it was just like yesterday our biological father had done everything possible to deny us the opportunity of being able to read and write? And now we were being punished severely by our foster mother for showing up at her home and not having the academic requirements children our ages should have. However, I do not believe for a moment that my foster mother's effort was driven by a compassionate outreach. Instead, I believe that she was merely concerned that we meet the basic academic requirements as stipulated by the CDA.

Despite the different philosophies, my brother and I had to adjust quickly to whatever environments we were subjected to. However, George was the one who paid the heavier price. Unfortunately, he was placed in a class that was being taught by my foster mother. I was terrified! No! Let me rephrase and reemphasize. I was extremely terrified!! I knew that, within a couple of months, I would be assigned to a class that was being taught by my foster mother. I could only imagine what it would be like for me if I had to spend an entire academic year being taught by her. I would definitely need several layers of rhino skin and a robotic mind to absorb the barrage of physical and psychological beating that she would have inflicted on me. Although I did not know much about prayer, for six months I prayed, hoped, and wished that I would never end up in a class that was being taught by my foster mother.

And Hallelujah! glory to God for answering my prayers. When it was all said and done, the following school year my foster mother was transferred from the third grade to the first grade. And come to think of it, my brother was a fast learner (from my perspective), and even then my foster mother made his life miserable throughout the six months he spent being taught by her. She not only punished him, but she did everything possible to humiliate him in the presence of his classmates.

For us to make it out of our respective grades, my brother and I had to adopt the forced learning approach rather than the usual progressive learning method. For example, we had to memorize exactly what was being taught because we did not have a basic academic foundation. As for me, I sketched out the information pixel by pixel. Or in a simpler computer term, I took screenshots of what was written on the blackboard. This is why I believe wholeheartedly that "A picture is worth a thousand words."

By the end of the school term, we had grasped the fundamentals necessary to move on to the next grade levels. I do not recall the exact headcount of my class; however, according to a copy of my class record located in my file at the CDA office, I was ranked fifth out of a total of fifty-six students. Ladies and gentlemen, I can assure you that from the day (December 9, 2009) I read that report, and even to this very day, I am still in a state of denial. However, if this is true, then I would like to classify this outcome as one of the greatest mysteries of our lifetime. Okay, let me be realistic because this result is more likely a gross oversight in which someone had forgotten to append the six so that my record would reflect a fifty-six out of a total of fifty-six students. Or could it be possible that only five students, including me, had shown up for the end-of-year exams? Well, I should not be leaning on my own understanding because with God, all things are possible.

I was quite curious to know my brother's class standing, so I read through his file thoroughly but was unable to locate his end-of-year class record. Irrespective of our end-of-year results and the learning techniques we had to apply, we were delighted to advance to the next grade levels. Well, our joy was short-lived because, by the start of the following school year, we were summoned back to our foster mother's traumatic academic boot camp.

On a more somber note, I would hope that this experience is viewed as a solemn but stern reminder for us, more so those of us who are parents. I would also hope that we realize that there are tremendous consequences for our actions, especially those that negatively affect the lives of the less fortunate children!

My foster father was not really involved in our lives that much. He was mostly a quiet person, except for a few occasional outbursts that sent shockwaves throughout the entire house. Occasionally, he would give George and me, floggings after receiving numerous complaints from our foster mother about our chores not being completed properly. She also complained that we were not coming home from the farm or school at the allotted time. I believe there were times when he would have given us a beating only if he had been able to catch us at that split second. We figured out that he could not run fast enough to catch us and he forgot easily. Well, as for the "forgot easily assertion," that was simply not the case. He was never a person to follow through on missed opportunities.

Here is a typical episode of how my brother and I would escape a beating whenever we did something such as not coming home from the farm at the designated time. Just to be clear, the extended time that we spent at the farm was mostly attributed to the fact that a number of the animals would escape from their enclosures and we had to round them up and carry out the necessary repairs. However, I must admit that there were times when, after taking care of the animals, George and I would go hunting for fruits in the nearby bushes or take a quick run to the clinic to have our wounds tended to by the nurse. Regardless of the reason, our foster mother would inform her husband of the time we had left, and the time we should have returned. She had all these time differences calculated down to the millisecond. To appease his wife, our foster father would give us a beating. However, many times he would make an effortless attempt to catch us but would give up the minute we took off running. And for him, that would be the end of the story.

Well, that was not always the case because one day, our foster father did chase after us, but it turned out to be an embarrassing situation for him. Here is how this dramatic episode unfolded. One day, George and I came home from the farm later than usual, most likely due to one of the reasons outlined above. Nonetheless, the minute we arrived, our foster mother said, "Desmond and George, a weh unnu did deh?" ("Desmond and George, where were you guys?") We did not answer because we knew that our foster mother would refute our explanation vigorously. Anyway, she turned to her husband and said, "Coltie, yuh a de man a de house. Do something because mi tiad fi talk to dem." ("Coltie, you are the man of the house. Do something because I am tired of talking to them.") Upon hearing those words, our foster father really wanted to show that he was the man of the house, so he came after us. We took off running and he kept coming after us like the Incredible Hulk. This became a real spectacle. That was when I heard our foster mother burst out with one of her usual gut-filled laughs, followed by, "Lawd Jeezas, look at de fat man running." ("Lord Jesus, look at the fat man running.") And as we would say in Jamaica, "Nu mek mi laugh till mi belly battam bus!" ("Do not make me laugh until my belly bursts!") Sure enough, my brother and I left him in the dust. He tried to diffuse the embarrassment by saying, "If mi did ever hab on mi shoes, unnu cudden get way fram mi." ("If I were wearing my shoes, you guys would not have gotten away from me.") Let's give him the benefit of the doubt because we all know that if he were wearing a pair of Usain Bolt sneakers, then the outcome would have been much different.

I hope you enjoy this little humor because this is one of the few incidents that make me laugh, even to this very day. Well, the laugh was on us when we had no way of escaping. In fact, I remember being beaten severely by my foster father to the point that I had visible marks all over my body. Once again, this was one of the instances in which our foster mother pressured him to take such action. I will fill you in on this episode later.

Sometimes it caused me to wonder why George and I were never in a hurry to return home. Although I do not have a definitive answer for this question, the one thing that I am sure of is this: being away from home provided us with temporary relief from the constant physical and psychological abuse. My brother was the recipient of our foster mother's severest forms of punishment, especially when he attempted to reason with her regarding her unfair treatment.

Returning home late was short-lived because our foster mother told us that we were not allowed to eat our dinner until all our chores were completed. Not only that, but she would leave our meals where they were accessible to the cats. In fact, any meal that was left unattended would undoubtedly become an open buffet for the pets, especially the two greedy cats. There were times when my brother and I would attempt to retrieve our meals from the kitchen before we completed our chores. However, our foster mother would chase us out of the kitchen like dogs.

Here is how such an event would unfold. After the chosen ones were all seated around the elegant dining table enjoying their meals, George and I would tiptoe into the kitchen, hoping to retrieve our meals before the greedy pets devoured them. However, with her keen sense of hearing and x-ray like vision, our foster mother would detect our presence and chase us out of the kitchen. Her actual words were, "Yes man, unnu creep in a di kitchen a look fi food like dawgs! Unnu naa get no food till unnu go tek care a di animals dem." ("Yes man, you guys sneaked into the kitchen looking for food like dogs! You are not getting any food until the animals are cared for.") With that said, my brother and I had to foot it several miles to and from the farms on empty stomachs and with minimal energy.

Up the Ante

After approximately three months of living with our foster parents, my brother and I had many stringent rules imposed on us. The first regimental rule was one that I remember quite vividly because it is permanently etched in my mind as if it happened yesterday. One day while I was entering the living room, my foster mother called my name, to which I answered the usual, "Yes, mummy." However, this day, her response was far different from what I was accustomed to. Immediately after my reply, she made a U-turn and started walking briskly toward me, thus causing us to become like two objects on a collision course. She met me at the doorway and started shouting at me in a loud and crude manner. With her finger wagging in my face, she said, "Never ever you address me as mummy again! You hear me! I am not your mother!" She went on to say, "Never you address another person who is not your mother as mummy either!" Upon hearing those words, I was devastated! I was terrified to the point that I found myself standing in the doorway in a daze long after she was gone.

At that moment, I felt heartbroken and began to question if all of the wonderful things that had been told to me by the CDA regarding going home to be with a family who had promised to be my loving and caring parents were really not true. Although this incident has made a permanent negative impression on me, it was quickly overshadowed by other unfolding events.

The second regimental rule that was imposed had to do with our accommodation and interaction with the rest of the family. The living room was off-limits, which was implied from the very first day we arrived. However, we were now explicitly told not to sit anywhere in the living room. This ruling was final because it did not matter if we had taken many showers and were dressed in our finest attire. My brother and I were quite familiar with our foster mother's swift "don't you dare" reaction whenever we attempted to defy any of her unjust rules. My foster parents and their adopted children were welcome to use these areas, however, my brother and I were not allowed. As for Barry, I had not seen him sitting on the couches or chairs (except for the Sunday morning's devotion) so I am not sure if he was told not to or this was his own decision.

As I alluded to earlier, not only was the living room off-limits but our royal treatment of sitting around the elegant dining room table also ended abruptly. Why could we no longer join the family at the dining table? Hadn't we mastered all aspects of our foster mother's table etiquette? Had we not showered and dressed in fine linen before joining the family for dinner? Okay, please disregard the fine linen comment, but I know you get the point I am conveying.

I cannot forget our reaction the day George and I walked into the dining room only to discover that our meals were not on the table. Just before we could inquire the reason, our foster mother intervened and, in a crude and derogatory manner, said, "Unnu si unnu food inna di kitchen. Tekkie an gu sidung outside pan di verandah." ("Your meals are in the kitchen. Take them and go and sit outside on the verandah.") In other words, our foster mother was informing us that we were no longer welcome to join the family at the dining table. This isolation rule was permanent because, from that day forward, we were never allowed to sit with the family at the dining table again, not even to enjoy a Christmas meal.

In addition to not being able to sit at the dining table, our foster mother did not care to inform us when our meals were served. However, we knew exactly when meals were served because we could hear the faint sounds coming from the chosen ones' utensils. This was a clear indication that they were seated at the elegant dining table, enjoying their meals. And, as I alluded to earlier, that was when George and I would tiptoe into the kitchen to retrieve our meals. However, as soon as we picked up the plates from the table, our foster mother would chase us out of the house like dogs.

The kitchen was sealed off from the rest of the house except for the curtains that hung between the kitchen and dining room, which were closed at mealtimes. This meant that no one was able to safeguard our meals from the pets. I believe it was those greedy cats who ate the large chicken breasts my foster mother would leave on our plates. Please forget I ever mentioned anything about chicken breasts because that would only be a mouth-watering dream on our part. In fact, the scraps such as the neck, back, the second and third tier of the wing, the gizzard, and the liver were the only parts of the chicken my brother and I were entitled to. The only exception was Christmas day when our foster mother would surprise us by adding a drumstick.

My foster mother did not only monitor every dime she had to spend, but our food portions were always on the meager side. However, we always had a way of making up the difference. First, we would eat the little leftovers, including the chicken bones, from our foster parents' plates. (In the words of an old KFC commercial, we literally "ate the bones!") Second, whenever we boiled the green bananas for the pigs, my brother and I used to eat some of that too. I know what you are thinking, but I am here to inform you that boiled green bananas are perfectly healthy for humans, not just pigs. Okay, if you don't believe me, then just search the internet and you will find all sorts of green banana recipes.

Not only was the living and dining room furniture off-limits for my brother and me but, clean or unclean, we were also barred from sitting on any of the chairs. Instead, we were told to sit on the floor behind a china cabinet that was located in the dining room. We also had to sit on the floor whenever we were allowed to watch television. Wouldn't life have been a lot more comforting for us if our foster parents had soft-padded, carpeted floors? I can assure you that there is absolutely no comfort for skinny people like us who had to sit on a tiled floor. Okay, I realize that I might be asking for too much but, in any case, a little rug would have sufficed.

The uncomfortable floor was not our only problem. In fact, while sitting on the floor and watching television, we had to make sure that we did not have our feet stretched out too much because if we did, our foster mother would kick us as she passed by. Although I use the word kick to describe her action, I do not believe that, in this instance, kicking us was her intent. I believe that this was her way of letting us know that we needed to scoot over or tuck in our feet. From our foster mother's perspective, we were occupying way too much floor space. Well, I must admit that there were times when we had our feet stretched out like we were at the beach basking in the sun. However, all this could have been avoided if we had been allowed to sit on a chair or the couch.

Another comfort that we were deprived of had to do with our sleeping arrangements. We were transferred from our comfy bed and had to share a little piece of foam on the floor. Sleeping on a piece of foam did not bother us because we were no strangers to this type of accommodation. I am merely reminiscing on the days George and I spent with our mother, as outlined in volume 1 of my autobiography. Shortly after that, my sleeping accommodation was upgraded when Maxwell (one of the boarders, whom I will bring into context shortly) was asked to share his twin-size bed with me. Well, prior to Maxwell's arrival that was our bed. However, that arrangement did not last for long because I was downgraded back to the little piece of foam on the floor due to a slight bed accident. Just to be clear, it was not Maxwell who caused the bed accident; it was me. I was the one who wet the bed, which was quite embarrassing for someone who was eleven-plus years old.

As it relates to those stringent isolationist measures, I believe firmly that my foster parents did everything possible to shun and marginalize my brother and me because we had many open wounds and emitted the stench of farm animals. If we made the mistake of going inside the house before we had taken a shower, we would be chased out like dogs. My brother and I were treated as outcasts. In fact, the other foster children were treated similarly, but not to the extent that George and I were. I will fill you in on the other foster children shortly.

However, the advantage of sitting on the outside meant that we no longer had to contend with our foster mother staring at us with bulging eyes, tapping on the table, or yelling at us whenever we slurped our soup or let the utensils make contact with our teeth. Let me not get ahead of myself, because we are well aware of the fact that every decision in life is associated with some form of unintended opportunity cost. With that in mind, I will now share with you the cost associated with eating our meals on the outside. Every day my brother and I were in constant battles with the dogs and the cats. Although we were quite careful, they would find a way to take our food right off our plates as if it were an open buffet. We were never given any trays, so it was quite a daunting task for us to balance the plates on our laps or on the narrow armrests of the little wooden bench and not end up spilling our meals.

On several occasions, the bowl or plate would slide right off the narrow armrest and shatter into several pieces when it made contact with the tiled floor. I remember my foster mother would yell at us from inside the dining room. Her most notable remark was, "Yes, man! Unnu stay deh anna mashup mi plate dem." ("Okay! You guys keep breaking my dishes!") She was not concerned about our meals spilling on the floor. Instead, she was more worried about her expensive china plates or bowls that we were breaking. After a few of these dish-breaking incidents, my foster mother bought two little plastic bowls that my brother I used for all of our meals from that point forward. Whether it was soup, rice, or porridge, the little plastic bowls became our designated meal containers.

As it pertained to the pets, it did not matter to them whether we were eating our meals from fine china or cheap plastic bowls, because they were always lurking around hoping for our meals to spill on the floor. The cats (Betty and Dinky) were the sneakier of the creatures we had to contend with. (And don't even ask about the names, because it was Michael who had assigned names to most of the pets, including the two cats.) Those two cats were quite clever. One would distract me from the right while the other would sneak up on my left. And the minute I moved my plate to the left or the right, the one or the other would snatch the little piece of meat right off my plate.

One particular afternoon, I was sitting on the little wooden bench enjoying my favorite meal. I believe it was Christmas Day, because that is the only time my brother and I would get a decent meal instead of the usual scraps. Anyway, that day I ate everything on my plate except the meat. That was deliberate because it was like saving the best for last. Just before I was through eating, I noticed that Betty and Dinky were up to their old tricks. Knowing that today's meal was special, I was certainly not about to let the two pesky cats outsmart me. Or at least that was what I thought. With that at the forefront of my mind, I took the chicken leg/drumstick from the plate and held it up high. I knew that Dinky was on my right, but I had no idea that Betty had slipped off to my left. And sure enough, with lightning speed and engineered precision, Betty defied gravity, leaped into the air, snatched the chicken leg out of my hand, and took off running. Boy, oh boy, was I upset! I got up and chased after her hoping that she would drop the chicken leg, but unfortunately, that was not her intention. That darn cat latched onto the chicken leg like a vice grip. And once again, I lost another one to Betty.

At any given time, there were at least four dogs and two cats at home. George and I were always in a constant battle throughout every meal, especially dinner. I have lost many food battles to those pets, especially the two cats who were continually lurking by or, in the words of a rapper, "always up in my grill." The moral of the story is this: whenever you find yourself outnumbered, outsmarted, and fully surrounded, then it's time for you to surrender.

The only time that I can recall not having to battle with those pets was when my foster mother poured cod liver oil all over my meal. One might ask why anyone would pour such smelly fish oil over someone's meal. At the time, I had no idea what nutritious value it provides, but I found out later that my foster mother did so as a way to build up my immune system because, in addition to my other illnesses, I was always coming down with the flu and fever. Knowing my foster mother, she was not too concerned about my health but was more concerned that my illnesses might cause her to incur unintended financial costs. Regardless of the reason, I was quite upset because I simply could not eat my meal with cod liver oil poured all over it. At such times I would throw my entire meal into the dogs' bowl, but not even the greedy pets would eat the food. I guess they did not have a need to build up their immune systems. In hindsight, I should have poured a little of the cod liver oil around the bench as a protective shield to repel the greedy pets. Come to think of it, the dogs and the cats rarely messed with Barry's meals. They knew that they would receive slaps whenever they attempted to snatch food off his plate. However, as for George and me, they could get away with pretty much anything because they realized that we were softies and pushovers. Okay, enough of the pet drama, let's highlight the other unpleasant events.

The third regimental rule that my foster mother enacted was to let my brother and me know that expressing our concerns and voicing our opinions were totally forbidden. She did not care to give a listening ear or even to have any form of conversation with us unless she was the one issuing the command. Looking at her in the face or making eye contact with her was also forbidden. On several occasions, we, more so my brother, would suffer dearly whenever we made the mistake of looking her directly in the face while she was speaking. We would receive a slap on the cheek, followed by a "Do not stare at me like that!" reprimand. I can assure you that this experience was very painful and frightening for us. I cannot begin to wonder what it must have been like for my brother, seeing that this was a regular ordeal for him. There were times when I could see the impression where my brother had been struck on his cheek by our foster mother.

Whenever we attempted to speak or explain ourselves, she would say, "Shut up! When an adult is speaking, you must be quiet." If we attempted to correct her regarding some form of accusation or unfair treatment, she would consider such action to be rude and disrespectful. In return, we would suffer grave consequences. By the way, "Children must remain quiet when an adult is speaking," is also a Jamaican philosophy; however, my foster mother took it to the extreme. In fact, it did not matter if she was speaking or not, we had to remain quiet and speak only in the affirmative of "yes, mam" or "no, mam" whenever she was addressing us. Some of the children who were aware of our regimented lifestyle would even use it to their advantage. They would pick on us, and there was nothing that we could do because they would say, "Yuh cyaa duh mi nutten cause mi wi mek yuh mada buss yuh ass." ("You cannot do anything to me because I will let your mother give you a beating.")

Here is a typical example that will further highlight the point I am conveying regarding my foster mother's total disregard for the well-being of the foster children. One of our daily chores included going to Mr. Campbell's sawmill to collect wood dust and wood scraps (sawdust and slabs according to Jamaicans) needed to replenish, build, or repair the animal and chicken enclosures. One particular Saturday afternoon, while my brother and I were at the sawmill toiling away gathering wood dust and wood scraps, all of a sudden a boy came by and started causing trouble. He was taking the wood scraps that we had worked so hard to separate from the scrap heap. I tried to stop him, but instead of realizing that he needed to "do the hard work" of gathering his own, he took a piece of the wood and smacked me right in my mouth, splitting my lower lip. After witnessing what had transpired, my brother chased the boy until he finally caught up with him in his yard. When he got hold of him, he threw him to the ground, while his mother and brothers looked on. I guess they were well aware that he was a troublemaker because neither his mother nor brothers retaliated, which was a bit surprising. That was the first and the last time that I ever saw my brother in such a rage.

The minute we got home with the many bags of wood dust and wood scraps, our foster mother came out to see if we were doing our chores. She noticed that I had a busted lip and a shirt that was partially drenched with blood. This unusual scene prompted her to ask, "What happened to you?" Seeing that I was experiencing difficulty speaking due to excruciating pain, my brother stepped in and told her that it was this troublemaker boy who had taken a piece of wood and hit me when we tried to stop him from taking our wood scraps. My foster mother looked at me and said, "Yes, man! Serve you right!" Then she went back inside the house. Out of everything that transpired that day, I am still disturbed by my foster mother's condescending response. She did not care to take a responsible approach and have a talk with this boy's parents. Instead, she assumed that my brother and I had gone to the sawmill and caused trouble, so whatever happened to us we were responsible.

The fourth regimental rule that my foster parents implemented came in the form of some of the severest punishment methods one could ever imagine. I would like to restate by saying that the foster children were the ones who were the recipients of my foster parents' physical punishment. In addition to the regular floggings, our punishment came in many forms that I would like to classify as the Devious Encounters. I have assigned labels as a way of differentiating among my foster parents' punishment methods. These were mostly my foster mother's punishment methods, but my foster father was just as responsible because he did very little to stop the outright abuse that was taking place right before his eyes.

Devious Encounters

- Corkscrew
- Vise Grip
- Head Bashing
- Knock, Knock on the Head
- Face Slapping
- Pinching, Tugging, and Wringing of the Ears
- Arm Punching
- Inhumane Flogging
- Stress-inducing Positions
  - Auto Pilot
  - Flamingo Pose
  - Kneeling Ritual
- Calorie Burner
- Night Shift
- Outsourcing

I will start out by explaining the Corkscrew method because, when compared to the others, this was the severest form of punishment. First, our foster mother would lock our heads under her arm, putting us in a headlock. Second, she would make a fist and wedge her knuckles against our foreheads. Finally, she would apply maximum pressure against our foreheads while turning her fist clockwise and counterclockwise. This form of punishment would cause a sharp pain to resonate from my forehead all the way to the back of my neck. After she was through, I would end up with a lump on my forehead and a severe headache that would last for several days.

As for the Vise Grip, she would bend her index and middle finger into the form of a hook and then use them to grip into our flesh while turning her hand in a clockwise direction. This is similar to being pinched harshly; however, my foster mother's enhanced method was so severe that it would radiate pain through my entire nervous system. Even for me with a very low percentage of body fat, she would still find a way to latch onto something.

As for the Head Bashing, my brother and I learned very early that our foster mother was quick on her feet and lethal with her hands! So whenever she summoned us to come and see her, we would try our best to stand at a safe distance away from her. However, that did not matter because she would say, "Come right here," and point to an area on the floor where we should stand. The minute we walked to the designated area, she would take our heads and bash them together like musical cymbals. There were times when our foster mother would sneak up behind us while we were sitting facing the opposite direction, grab our heads, and bash them together so hard it felt as though my head was about to explode. In addition to the pain, for a split second, it appeared as though I was seeing a million twinkling stars. Or in the words of a Jamaican, I was seeing peeny wallies (insects that glow in the dark, similar to fireflies).

Throughout such times, George could not help but stomp his feet on the ground and raise his voice at her by saying, "Mam! Why mam!? Why!?" She was not deterred by our cries or any of my brother's pleas. As a matter of fact, she appeared to have enjoyed doing this because she would burst out into one of her gut-filled laughs whenever she witnessed my brother and I running away while holding our heads due to the excruciating, lingering pain that followed. After she was through laughing, she would say, "Yes man, serve unnu right, all unnu du a nyam and sidung." ("Yes man, serve you guys right because all you do is eat and then sit down.") She resorted to these disciplinary measures as a way of reminding us that after we were through eating, we should get busy with our chores instead of sitting down. I am not sure what she meant because most of the times we had to complete all our chores before we were allowed to eat our meals. Nonetheless, our foster mother did not want to see us sitting down and not working.

Here is a little side note as it relates to the head-bashing I outlined above. By enduring many of these painful head bashings, I came to realize that the very tip of the ear is one of the most sensitive areas of the body. There were times when my foster mother would bash our heads together and the tips of my ears would end up receiving most of the impact. Ladies and gentlemen, that would cause severe pain to radiate throughout my entire body. Now that I think about it, I wish we had a pair of NFL football helmets to protect ourselves from all those head bashings.

So what is this Knock, Knock on the Head form of punishment? This would occur mostly during our study sessions. Our foster mother would make a fist and use her knuckles to hit us repeatedly on our foreheads whenever we were experiencing difficulties reading, solving math problems, or using correct grammar. At the end of the study session, we would end up with lumps (coco, as per Jamaicans) on our foreheads. We had no way of minimizing our punishment because we had no idea what set of math problems we would be asked to solve or what books our foster mother would have us read. In fact, she did not provide us with a copy of the required textbooks, which meant we were unable to do any preparatory work.

Being quite slow academically, I would end up with the biggest lump on my forehead at the end of the study session. Not only that, but I would compound my misery because every time that I was summoned by my foster mother to stand before her, my heartbeat would go into overdrive, my vision would get blurred, my hands and feet felt numb, and my brain would eventually shut down. Come to think of it, I would be considered a very fluent reader just before I was summoned by my foster mother to stand before her and read aloud. Okay, please omit the words "very fluent" from the previous statement because my reading sounded more like a sputtering motor. The point is that I ended up receiving most of the abuse because my learning progress was very slow. Not only that but my reading and comprehension skills were compounded by extreme fear, thus causing me to become an irritant to my foster mother. In addition to enduring her many forms of physical abuse, her terrifying screams such as, "For the last time! The word is . . . !" were all I could hear echoing in my ears.

As the label implies, Face Slapping was when our foster mother would slap or hit us (sometimes with a closed fist) on our cheeks because we had made the mistake of making eye contact with her while she was speaking or we had said something that she deemed out of place or ill-mannered. Although I was seldom hit with a closed fist, it was my brother who suffered most of this abuse. The imprint on my brother's cheek was a clear indication that he had been hit with a closed fist. It was devastating to see my brother crying while holding his cheek due to the blows that our foster mother had inflicted on him.

As for the Pinching, Tugging, and Wringing of the Ears, we learned quite early that the less we were in our foster mother's presence, the less likely that we would end up being punished. Many times we would run and hide when we heard our foster mother yelling our names. One of her most notable remarks was, "Desmond and George, unnu cyaa run, but unnu cyaa hide, so unnu stay deh a run, yuh hear." ("Desmond and George, you guys can run, but you cannot hide, so keep on running.") By hiding and not responding to her calls, we would only make matters worse because as soon as we found ourselves within arm's reach of our foster mother, she would give us a couple of whacks, followed by a constant tugging, pinching, and wringing of our ears. She would do this while repeating, "George and Desmond, unnu nuh hear mi wen mi a call unnu?") ("George and Desmond, you guys did not hear me calling you?")

This form of punishment was not only exclusive to the times we tried to hide from our foster mother. In fact, she would inflict similar punishment on us throughout her boot-camp study sessions. I despised this form of punishment because I was always the recipient due to my inability to learn at my foster mother's desired pace. And woe unto the child (I was always that child) whose lack of understanding caused my foster mother to repeat herself. Whenever she was through tugging, pinching, crushing, and twisting my ear, I would feel intense pain followed by a burning sensation. It felt as though my ear was on fire. Also, a day or two later, I would hear a constant thumping sound in my ears. Not to mention the times when yellow fluid would ooze out of my ear for several days. This side effect turned out to be my most annoying ear discomfort. I had to stuff my ear with tissue paper to prevent the fluid from leaking out while I was at church and school. I am not sure if my foster mother's constant tugging, pinching, crushing, and twisting of my ears was the cause for my ear infections. However, there was no way of telling because for the entire time my brother and I spent with our foster parents, we never had a doctor visit or a health checkup.

The Arm Punching method of punishment occurred whenever our foster mother caught us taking a piece of food or a snack that had not been given to us. She would punch us repeatedly on our arms while repeating one of her usual phrases, "Yes man, a dis yah a get yuh inna trouble." ("Yes man, this is what is getting you into trouble.") This was a very painful method of punishment because the muscle on my arm that was being punched would ebb and flow. I am not sure how else to describe the effect, but it reminded me of the rising tide of the ocean. My arm would be in severe pain for several days. Even to this day, I am still trying to figure out why my foster mother would resort to such a drastic measure when all we had done was to take a little snack that had not been given to us. Probably this was her way of disarming the suspects.

I know you might be asking yourself, why not just ask instead of taking food or snacks that had not been given to you? We did ask, but our foster mother's reply was always, "No! You do not deserve any!" or, "Did you provide any?" Therefore, we decided to take the riskier but sometimes more rewarding approach by helping ourselves to a snack. My foster mother's "Ask and it shall not be given unto thee" policy reminded me of a little phrase I learned while living at the orphanage, where food was always a scarce commodity. It goes something like this: "Who beg nah get, who nuh beg nuh want." The English translation is, "Those who ask shall not receive, and those who do not ask, do not need." Therefore, whichever way you look at it, you are simply out of luck.

Inhumane Flogging is when our foster parents, more so our foster mother, used leather straps, garden hose, and sticks to beat the children, mostly, the foster children. The elaborate process my foster mother went through to acquire those enhanced leather straps and the time and effort she exerted to prepare the many pieces of sticks and garden hoses, caused me to wonder what was going on in her mind. Why were my foster parents in need of so many beating devices? As I ponder over their actions, I found myself wondering if at any time throughout the process they had realized that their actions towards the children were inhumane. Even to this day, I find myself asking if my former foster parents had ever consider the consequences of their actions.

If my foster mother were not in the mood to dish out any physical punishment, she would still inflict pain on us by subjecting us to her stress-inducing forms of punishment. The three most prominent ones were the Auto Pilot, Flamingo Pose, and Kneeling Ritual. These forms of punishment are similar to a "timeout." However, in this context, we would have to stand or kneel in the corner with our arms stretched out directly in front of us or stand on one leg, while at the same time using our left hands to hold our right ears or vice versa. At first, I thought these punishment methods were easy or, should I say, the lesser of the evils when compared to the physical beatings. However, after my first encounter, I had to move these methods up one notch on the PainOmeter scale. There were times throughout this punishment phase when we would have liked to give our arms or feet a rest, but we dared not let our foster mother see us lowering, raising, or wobbling our arms or feet as though we were experiencing some form of turbulence. If we did, we would most certainly have our punishment time extended by another fifteen to twenty minutes. And let me emphasize, having our punishment time extended by even five minutes was like waiting for an eternity to expire!

Another one of my foster mother's punishment methods came in the form of what I would describe as the Calorie Burner. Although our foster parents had two vehicles (a minivan and a car, to be precise), George and I had to walk approximately seven miles to and from school, mostly barefooted. My foster mother's vehicle could carry at least six people, and she taught at the very same school we attended, but we still had to walk to and from school. While walking home, we would observe as our foster mother drove by in the HOV lane in her big blue station wagon Ford Cortina car, leaving us behind. Well, the above statement is correct except for the HOV lane reference. Actually, those narrow winding country roads could barely accommodate two vehicles going in the opposite directions, much less accommodate HOV lanes. The point is, she would swoosh by in her spacious car, leaving us behind as if we were unknown hitchhikers. Even though George and I were not allowed to ride in the car, we still had to make sure that it was cleaned from rim to roof, inside and outside.

I must also emphasize that on the rare occasions when my brother and I were allowed to ride in the car, our foster mother would find the most trivial reasons to justify ending our rides prematurely. Here is how one of these episodes would unfold. Instead of walking to school like we normally would, my brother would make a desperate plea to our foster mother to please provide us with a ride because we were exhausted from the overwhelming amount of work that we had to do that morning. The excess work would be attributed to the fact that a number of the animals had escaped from their enclosures and we had to round them up and then perform the necessary repairs. After hearing such a compelling justification, our foster mother would allow us to ride in the car with the family (most of the time it would be just her and her adopted son) that morning. So, there we were, seated comfortably in the car on our way to school. However, approximately one mile into the journey (I still remember the exact location), the sun's rays reflected on the car windshield and revealed a few watermarks that had not been visible to us while it was in the garage. As soon as our foster mother noticed that the windshield was not spotless, she stopped the car and said, "George and Desmond, unnu cum outa de car." ("George and Desmond, get out of the car.") Sure enough, that was where our comfortable ride would end, and we had no other choice but to foot the rest of the journey.

If you think that just walking the rest of the way to school was the last of our troubles, then to that I say, think again. Back in those days, the principal would punish (by a physical beating) the children for being tardy. My brother and I were guaranteed a beating because it was quite difficult for us to complete all our morning chores and get to school on time. Anyway, it was not a pleasant outcome for us when we ran all the way to school only to see the principal standing at the main entrance with a leather strap dishing out punishment. We could hear the screams from the children being punished echoing all the way down the street. The most frightening ordeal was for my brother and me to see our foster mother standing with the principal at "hell's" gate, beckoning to us to come and receive our flogging. She was there to inform the principal that my brother and I were tardy and should be punished. She made it appear as though we had all the opportunity in the world to get to school on time, but instead had chosen to be tardy. And with her standing there, we were unable to explain to the principal the reason why we were unable to get to school on time. Every time that I reflect on this injustice, I find myself asking why my foster mother would create such an impression when she knew that she was the sole reason why my brother and I were unable to get to school on time. The principal did not care to find out the reason why my brother and I had to walk to school while our foster mother drove a car and taught at the very school we attended.

The only time that my brother and I were guaranteed a ride to school was when our foster father had to take the family to school because one of the vehicles was being serviced by the mechanic. On those days, instead of walking to school like we normally would, George and I would get ready for school and stand by the vehicle. As soon as the rest of the family was about to get into the vehicle, my foster mother would notice that my brother and I were standing off to the side, waiting for a ride.

In a very crude manner, she would rebuke us by saying, "George and Desmond, unnu si di road deh. Unnu nah drive inna di vehicle!" ("George and Desmond, there is the road. You guys are not riding with us in the vehicle!") Immediately after that, our foster father would get really upset and say, "George and Desmond, unnu get inside the vehicle, yuh hear mi?" ("George and Desmond, you guys get inside the vehicle, you hear me!") With that said, my brother and I would be guaranteed a ride to school that morning, but not without taking a verbal beating from our foster mother. For the entire journey, she would say things like, "Yes man, a Coltie a mek unnu get weh wid everyting. A im a bruck unnu bad." ("Yes, Coltie is allowing you guys to get away with everything. He is the one spoiling you guys.")

Before I finalize the car episode, I would like to take this opportunity to say a big thank you to Mrs. Belford, my fifth-grade teacher, for giving George and me a ride to school whenever she had just enough space in her car to squeeze us in. Although her car (Hillman Hunter: Sunbeam AKA Roots as per Jamaicans) was much smaller than that of my foster mother, and she had to transport her two sons and sometimes a coworker or two, she would try her best to provide us with a ride even if we had to stand in the little space between the front and the rear seats. I must also extend the same to her husband for providing us with a ride in the back of his pickup truck when he took his family to school. I am quite sure that they did not approve of my foster mother's not allowing my brother and me to ride in the car with the rest of the family. However, what I am most humbled by is the fact that Mr. and Mrs. Belford would still give us a ride in their vehicles regardless of how may open wounds we had or how sweaty and smelly we were. Well, Mr. Belford did not have to worry about our body odor because having us ride in the back of his pickup truck must have been a "Febreze." By the way, in reference to the Stewart Town All-Age School, throughout such time, only the principal, Mrs. Belford, and my foster mother owned motor vehicles.

After a while, my brother and I did not mind walking to and from school, at least throughout the cool months. The most dreaded of all times was when the parish council repaved the road, and we had to walk home from school barefooted. Throughout such times, especially the days leading up to summer, the melted asphalt would bubble to the surface, and if we happened to step on any of those areas, we would certainly feel the heat radiating throughout our "soles." However, my brother and I learned to adapt. That is, instead of walking the entire way home on the hot asphalt, we would take all the available alternate paths through the woods.

Walking to and from school was even more daunting when we had to walk on the side, heel, or tips of our toes; the reason being that we had suffered severe cuts or piercing wounds on the bottoms of our feet. This was mostly caused by broken bottles, nails, or other piercing objects that were scattered all over the farms and the backyard.

After a while walking home from school was no longer a matter of just getting home, but what time our foster mother was expecting us to be home. That is, after a couple of days of getting home on our timeframe, our foster mother demanded that we get home much earlier. Her exact words were, "George and Desmond, ih shudden tek unnu dis lang fi get home." ("George and Desmond, it should not have taken you guys this long to get home.") With that said, my brother and I had to run home as quickly as possible. Not only that, but our foster mother would be on the lookout to see where we were whenever she drove by in her spacious Ford Cortina station wagon. She wanted to have a clear indication of where we were and how long it should have taken us to get home. If we did not get home in the allotted time, she would give us a stern reprimand. She would say something to the effect of, "George and Desmond, I passed you guys at point 'x', and it should have taken you guys 'y' time to get home. So, how is it that you are just getting home?" We would remain very quiet because we had no idea how to apply Newton's law of motion, much less to quantify speed, time, and distance algebraic equations. Now that she was on a constant lookout for us, we could no longer use our alternate paths through the woods.

I remember how angry she got the first time she drove by while we were on our way through the woods like Little Black Riding Hoods. The minute we got home, she started huffing and puffing at us like the big bad wolf. She said, "George and Desmond, a how mi pass an nuh si unnu? A weh unnu did deh?" ("George and Desmond, how is it that I passed by but did not see you guys? Where were you guys?") Then she would continue by accusing us of going to people's homes or some other places where we should not have been.

In retrospect, it is quite difficult for me to believe that a few petty things, such as watermarks on the windshield, were the sole reasons why our foster mother was very reluctant to let us ride in the vehicle. I believe that our physical hygiene, as a result of being amongst the farm animals, and our open wounds were the main reasons why we were not allowed in the vehicle. This rationale would also explain why we were shunned at all times and not allowed to join the family at the dining table not even on special occasions. It also explains why we were forced to sleep on a piece of foam on the floor and told to sit on the floor, mostly behind a cabinet away from the rest of the family. The reason why we had to hand wash our clothes in a separate washbasin instead of in the washing machine with the rest of the family's laundry.

The next form of punishment is one I describe as the Night Shift. George and I used to dread the summer holidays because our foster mother would "turn up the heat" on us and dish out the severest forms of punishment. I can assure you that my foster mother was like our worst Madam Kryptonite. Whenever she noticed that we were taking a break, she would find something wrong or something out of place that would cause her to give us beatings or head bashings as I alluded to earlier. I believe that her philosophy was that we should be working at all times, even throughout the night.

I know it may sound a little extreme, but this is where I will explain what I mean by the term Night Shift. Once upon a summer night, just as George and I were about to retire to bed, we were summoned by our foster mother to come to her right away. We were bracing for a beating, but in this instance, that was not the case. Instead, she said, "Unnu a guh a wok wid Coltie fi mek unnu si how hard im haffi wok fi feed unnu." ("You guys are going to accompany Coltie to his workplace so that you can experience how hard he has to work to feed you.") Wow! In hindsight, I do not believe for a minute that our small portion of food was the reason why Coltie had to work that hard! Weighing somewhere around three hundred pounds, I believe wholeheartedly that Coltie was working very hard to feed himself.

I must admit that, for the first couple of nights, it was more like a fun-packed adventure than a form of punishment. So what exactly did we do all night while we accompanied our foster father to the different Kaiser Bauxite mining sites? For the first couple of hours, we had the opportunity of riding around in the pickup truck with our foster father and observing as he supervised the workers who were stationed at the different mining locations.

First he took us to the train depot, placed us on one of the trains, and told the train operator that we would be staying with him for a couple of hours. We observed the train operator as he towed the railcars to the loading dock. After the first railcar was filled with ore, he would repeat the process by towing another, then another, and so on. In other words, his designated job was to tow railcars to the loading dock for the duration of his work shift. After the first hour of watching the same repetitive process, I was more than ready for a transfer. I believe the train operator enjoyed our company, because he took the time to explain the entire mining operation to us.

After a couple of hours, our foster father returned, took us to another location, and placed us in one of the gigantic earth-mining machines located deep in the ground. He left us with the operator for another two to three hours. The operator told us to address him as Lucky. And as the name implies, I believe anyone who operates equipment that deep in the ground and is not swallowed up by many tons of ore should, indeed, be considered lucky. Actually, there were times when it appeared as though everything was about to come crashing down on us. We watched as Mr. Lucky mined the ore and loaded it onto the gigantic trucks that hauled it from the site back to the train depot. He also explained the mining process to us. Not only did Mr. Lucky enjoyed our company, but he was happy to share his snacks with us as well. I will not bore you with all of the details, but instead, will make them available in my next book, which will be titled "Lucky and the Giant Machine."

Okay, I have veered a little too far off the topic, so let's get back to the Night Shift operation. After spending approximately six hours being shuttled to and from different mining sites, our foster father took us back to his vehicle and told us to take naps. Finally, in the morning, somewhere around 8:00 a.m., he provided us with a cup of tea. After he was through working, we departed the job site and went home.

The minute we got home, George and I had to get going with the farm chores because there were lots of hungry animals and chickens to be cared for. One would think that after working the Night Shift, George and I would be allowed to take the rest of the day off. No sir! There was simply no rest for the weary. In hindsight, my brother and I should have asked Coltie to give us a hand with the farm chores so that he could experience how hard *we* had to work to feed *him*.

I do believe that accompanying our foster father to his job would have been a noble cause if our foster mother's intention had been to provide us an opportunity to bond with our foster father rather than using it as a form of punishment. I do not object to the idea of children having first-hand experiences of their parents' job responsibilities. I also believe such an experience would help children become more appreciative of the sacrifices being made on their behalf.

My foster mother's final punishment method came in the form of what I describe as Outsourcing. Just when George and I thought that our summer workload could not have gotten any harder, once again our foster parents proved us wrong. One day after we were through with our farm chores, we were summoned by our foster mother to go to the home of an elderly couple, who were church members, to assist them with their farm duties. My foster parents were indeed exercising the *workhouse* principle.[4] After incurring a four-mile walk to the church members' home, we would spend many hours threshing beans the old-fashioned way.

For those of you who are not familiar with this manual process, it involves six basic steps.

First, you harvest the beans by pulling up the plants from the soil. Second, you place the harvested plants on a tarpaulin and let them stay in the sun for a couple of hours. Third, after the pods are dried to a crisp, you place the plants, including the pods, into a bag. Fourth, you hit or beat the bag with a stick until the beans are separated from the pods. Fifth, you remove both the beans and the trash from the bag and separate the excess trash from the beans. Sixth and final, you apply a wind sifting method by throwing the beans and the remaining trash into the air to allow the wind to separate the trash from the beans.

---

4 To put this statement in context, please refer to Appendix A, Orphans in the Predated and Postdated Eras of the Foster Care System.

Speaking from personal experience, if you grow a lot of beans, then I would suggest that you get a bean separator. Please do not resort to this backbreaking, manually intensive process. Hmmm, come to think of it, I wonder if my foster parents were being compensated but kept the proceeds to themselves. Irrespective of George and I not being paid, we did enjoy the all-you-can-eat buffet meals the family would provide us.

The church brother and his wife were so impressed with our work ethics, he requested our help many times after that. Well, I must admit that it was my brother's hard work that impressed them the most. In hindsight, I wonder if this church brother had thought that just because my brother and I were living with a well-to-do family it meant that we were sitting at home all summer playing Nintendo Wii, PlayStation, and Xbox video games. Okay, please erase video game systems from your memory because we had no such things.

It appeared as though George and I were constantly fighting against all of the earth's natural elements. Well, it was more like four of the elements: earth, water, wind, and our foster mother. Whenever it rained, we had to remove the excess water from all the open areas, such as the verandahs, garage, and walkways. As for the wind, we had to make sure that we had a broom within reach at all times because as soon as the wind blew a couple of leaves or loose soil onto the paved areas, we had to sweep it off right away. Even if everything was in place and all our chores were completed, our foster mother would notice that a meteorite was on the ground and that was when she would shout at us, "George and Desmond, what is that meteorite doing on the ground?" Despite my over-the-top dramatization, I do believe you get the point that it was in our interest to remain vigilant at all times. If our foster mother noticed that these chores were not done promptly and to her satisfaction, we would be punished severely. For those reasons, I would pray for the summer break to end. I am quite sure the other foster children felt the same way. Our minds, bodies, and souls were at peace only during the times our foster mother was away from home, even if it was only for an hour.

Beating Apparatus

To inflict even more physical and psychological pain on us, our foster mother would stockpile many types of beating apparatus. She would summon my brother or me to cut branches from a crape myrtle plant (June rose, as per Jamaicans). She would use the sticks to inflict much pain and suffering unto the foster children. She would also take a number of the smaller crape myrtle sticks with her to school and use them to punish the children. One day a man saw a number of these nicely shaped sticks protruding out of her bag and, being quite curious, asked, "Lady, what are you going to do with those sticks?" I remember my foster mother replied sarcastically, "You went to school, you should know what they are for." The man became indignant, and a heated exchange erupted between him and my foster mother. It was obvious that he was quite upset to know that my foster mother was using those sticks to punish the children. If this man was upset with her because he perceived that she was about to use those sticks to abuse the children, then can you imagine what his reaction would have been if he had stopped by my foster parents' home and witnessed her extensive collection of lethal beating apparatus? In this situation, my foster mother should not have been alarmed because any person of sound mind and impartial judgment would definitely have been concerned with her response and the intended consequences as it related to the children.

By the way, when pruned occasionally, crape myrtle grows many long and sturdy branches, as indicated by the images that are included. Speaking from experience, I can assure you that from my foster mother's perspective, these branches were the ideal beating apparatus. At first, I thought that this was one of my foster parents' GMO plants. However, I was proven wrong when many years later, I saw it scattered across the landscape of Florida and North Carolina. Not only that, but while I was living in North Carolina, this plant was all over the complex and even by my bedroom window. Would you believe that whenever I would go jogging those crape myrtle trees would reach out and give me a good whack? Okay, as for the crape myrtle's giving me a whack, that's pure dramatization on my part. Nonetheless,

This is what crape myrtle trees look like when they are occasionally pruned. Picture date: 2010.

The crape myrtle tree that stood directly outside my window. Not only that, but when the wind blew, the branches would rub against the gutter and make a creepy, scary sound. Picture date: 2010.

even though this plant brings back painful childhood memories, I am still fascinated by its tranquil bloom! However, if you wish to send me flowers, please send me a rose, not June rose.

Garden hose was the next beating apparatus that my foster mother used to abuse the foster children. She would cut an entire 50-, 75- or 100-foot garden hose into several pieces approximately two and a half to three feet long and add them to her beating apparatus stockpile. We suffered countless beatings with those pieces of garden hose. The hose would leave visible swollen marks all over our bodies. I was terrified by the scary swooshing sound coming from the hose when my foster mother was using it to punish us.

In addition to the sticks and garden hose, the next beating apparatus was my foster mother's lethal leather straps, which I dubbed the Snake. I refer to this description because it was always coiled and ready to strike at any moment. I would like to emphasize by saying that this was surely not a pleasant sight for the foster children to behold. The leather straps were custom-made by a local leatherworker and were approximately two and a half to three feet long. The leatherworker had either stitched or glued several layers of leather together to provide the desired thickness. To either preserve the leather or to give it the desired weight and lethalness, my foster mother or the leatherworker would soak it in a type of oil-based solution. (I heard that this oil-based solution was diesel fuel. However, I am not sure because neither my foster mother nor the leatherworker ever revealed the process of what it took to transform leather into such a lethal device.)

As I reminisce about this experience, I am beginning to wonder if this leatherworker had ever realized that there could be no possible justification for these devices other than to bring about physical and psychological harm to the children who had been placed in the care of my foster parents. It definitely was not a belt, because it did not include the most basic components and features, such as a buckle and the designated holes. Therefore, I wonder if this person had ever realized that his craftsmanship was promoting and, in many respects, enhancing the abusive behaviors of my foster parents, mostly those directed at the foster children who had been placed in their care. Or could it be that this person was not deterred simply because he was not the one using this device to bring about harm to a child? I also believe that the monetary incentive had marred the conscience of this person to the point that he was willing to overlook all the tangible evidence that was right before his eyes.

My foster parents did not deem it important to provide us with basic medical care or even to purchase protective shoes for us to wear while working in the maggot-infested chicken coops and pigpens. However, they could justify spending all that money on custom-made beating devices. Think about how many pairs of protective shoes could have been purchased with the money that they were spending on things that had no other purpose than to bring about physical and psychological harm to the inno-cent. Not only that, but many years later, I discovered that my foster parents had written to the CDA complain-ing that they were not being compensated enough.

I can assure you that it was certainly not a pleasant sight witnessing my foster mother preparing and stockpil-ing those punishment devices. Why was she in need of so many punishment devices? We, the foster children, were terrified just to be in the presence of our foster mother. She did not need to have a beating device at her disposal so that she could subject us to physical pain. I remember one day while my brother and I were in the kitchen toiling away at our chores, my foster mother directed one of her hurtful and degrading remarks at my brother, like she usually did. Although I did not hear the exact words, it must have touched my brother's most sensitive nerve because it caused him to mumble out something a bit too loudly for our foster mother's ears. Regardless of what the exchange was, within the twinkling of an eye, I saw my foster mother rush into the kitchen, corner my brother like a boxer, and start punching him repeatedly. Even when my brother fell onto the floor and was in a helpless state, she was not deterred. She pinned him to the floor with her knees and kept pounding him with her fists, while repeating, "George, a manhandle yuh want, an a manhandle yuh a get." ("George, you need to be manhandled, and I am manhandling you.")

This episode is one of my most painful and fearful childhood memories and one that lingers in my memory. Throughout this whole ordeal, I was terrified to the point that I broke out in a cold sweat. I wanted to make a mad dash out of the kitchen, but I could not because it felt as though I had no life in my feet. Even to this very day, I find it quite difficult to understand why a person who claimed to be of sound mind would inflict so much pain and suffering unto an innocent child! For what? Only because my brother dared to let her know that she should not address us as dogs and scavengers, and that she should stop abusing the children!

This incident caused me to wonder how many times my brother had been dragged off into the "dark" halls of our foster parents' house and abused in such a manner. I tried to convince George that he could minimize his affliction by remembering that silence was always his best response. However, today I realize that I was asking my brother to compromise his human dignity. Besides, he was reminding me that it is ok to speak out against injustice, irrespective of the costs.

As time progressed, my brother and I developed an overwhelming fear of our foster mother. We would try our best to stay out of her sight as much as we possibly could. Actually, we would camp out at the back of the house or at the far end of the property just to be out of her sight. We were extremely terrified whenever she would summon us to come to her. She would say in a very stern and crude manner, "George and Desmond, unnu come to me right now!" We would start crying without even knowing the reason why we had been summoned in the first place. Then she would say, "Unnu stay de a ball til mi gi unnu somting fi ball fah." ("You guys stay there crying, I might just give you something to cry about.") Many times, I was so scared and felt like I was about to pee my pants. It was not just my brother and me who were terrified of our foster mother. In fact, there were times when the lava of her wrath would spill over and even her adopted son, Michael, would start crying when she summoned him.

I do not want to give the impression that every time that we were punished it was unwarranted. With that in mind, here are two instances in which we would indulge in behaviors that would put us at odds with our foster mother. First, with so many children in the home and with boys being boys, there were times when we would have silly arguments, mostly over the ownership of things. George and I would end up being punished severely because we just could not resist playing with Michael's toys when he was not present. (Michael was the only child who received Christmas presents. In fact, none of the foster children received any gifts, which was a cause for an occasional childish argument.)

Second, there were times when George and I would sneak out of the house and go hunting for fruits to quell the hunger. Mmm yummy, I can still taste those delicious guavas and guineps we used to harvest from the property across the street. As I alluded to earlier, there were times when the hunger would become unbearable and we could not resist taking snacks from the refrigerator or the pantry without our foster mother's consent. I am still amazed by my foster mother's keen sense with regard to food. She would notice that a slice of bread, $\frac{1}{16}^{th}$ inch of cake, or one whole chicken wing was missing. Well, as for the chicken wing, that's an easy one to spot. Actually, I have a somewhat hilarious drama that I would like to share with you.

Without further delay, here comes the "who stole my wing" drama. Once upon a bright and sunny Sunday morning, a mysterious force lured me a little too close to my foster mother's kitchen and I happened to smell the irresistible, sweet aroma of fried chicken in the air. On that particular morning, I was quite hungry and the temptation of taking a piece of the chicken from the pot was one I simply could not resist. Before I could think about the consequences, I went into the kitchen, snatched one whole chicken wing from the pot, and devoured it. What was I thinking? I had temporarily forgotten about my foster mother's eagle eyes and elephantine memory. The minute she opened the pot, she noticed that one of the chicken wings was missing. Well, that was obvious, because it would be highly unlikely for a chicken to have only one wing. I was the first to be summoned to the investigation room. My foster mother pried my mouth open, and the evidence was overwhelming. The only thing that was missing was the chicken feathers. Anyway, she said, "Desmond, come here, come and kneel down in the corner by the stove." Not only did I have to kneel by the stove, but my foster mother took a big pumpkin from the basket, placed it on my head, and told me to hold it in place.

I guess she wanted me to hold the pumpkin on my head while she carved it for Halloween. Okay, please disregard the Halloween reference, but you get the point that my foster mother was a very masterful punishment improviser. Today I can treat this episode as one big comical drama but at the time, kneeling down beside a stove with hot stuff all around was indeed a very terrifying ordeal. However, the punishment did not end there because I was not given any meat with my dinner that Sunday afternoon and for several more meals. This no-meat experience had me wondering if my foster mother had adopted my father's ital diet. Anyway, I learned a valuable lesson: never to treat my foster mother's pot as if it were an open buffet.

Here are two other instances in which I was punished, and rightfully so. The first incident happened while I was at school, with too much time on my hands. Instead of using such precious time to catch up on my studies (which I needed to do because of my slow learning deficiency), I decided to clown around. There I was, sitting on the pavement across from the third-grade classroom, using a rubber band to shoot objects at random targets. And guess what? The unthinkable happened when one of the objects went hurtling through the air and landed squarely on a third-grader's cheek.

I can never forget the boy whose cheek was hit. His name was Stanley. In hindsight, this little boy reminded me of Chicken Little. For him, the sky was always falling. I mean, he cried for everything. He cried for a whole day because someone accidentally knocked over the container with his show-and-tell pet fish.

As soon as the object hit him on his cheek, he went screaming to his teacher as if he had just gotten all his teeth knocked out. Without any hesitation, all fingers were pointing squarely at me. Right then and there, I could see the rest of my day getting gloomier by the minute. Sure enough, a complaint was lodged with my foster mother. I looked up and, behold, I saw my foster mother coming down the corridor like a wrestler being tagged and about to enter the ring. Foreseeing the wrath that was about to be unleashed on me, I got up quickly, ran to my classroom, and sat quietly in my seat pretending not to be the guilty party. However, that did not ward off the wrath that was coming down on me. My foster mother marched into the classroom, picked me up out of my seat by my shirt collar, and dragged me approximately seventy-five feet along the corridor to her classroom, while the curious children looked on. That day she used one of her lethal leather straps and gave me one of the worst beatings anyone could ever imagine. Not only was I severely beaten, but I was told to stand at the front of her class before all the children for approximately three hours.

The second and final incident happened on a day when the entire school was getting ready to participate in the annual school sporting competition. With no teacher present in my classroom, I decided to commence the celebration a little too early. I saw Bryon, one of my classmates, eating dried powdered milk out of his hand and, in a jovial manner, I hit his hand in an upward motion causing his powdered milk to go airborne. Byron did not find this prank funny, so he reacted and a little game of tag-like pushing and shoving broke out between us.

The last thing I remember was when he shoved me and took off running. However, just like bad luck, Byron tripped and hit his head on a concrete basin that was located at the back of the classroom. The incident traveled to my foster mother faster than the speed of sound. That day, I experienced a double dose of my foster mother's wrath because she had incurred a cost for Byron's doctor visit. And, ladies and gentlemen, woe unto the child whose action caused my foster parents to incur any unwarranted financial cost.

Although I did not know much about prayer, I prayed fervently that Byron was ok and that time would go by quickly. As part of my punishment, I was not allowed to attend school for the remainder of the week. However, when I inquired of my brother how Byron was doing, he assured me that Byron was doing well because he had seen him at school playing with his classmates. I can assure you that this was a big "Hallelujah! Thank you, Jesus" moment for me!

Just when I thought the Byron incident was finally behind me, my punishment was compounded when my foster mother said to me, "Dat's right, a tell Mr. Nelson fi put yuh name inna di logbook and fi dat, yuh nah come out to nuttin good inna life." ("That's right, I told Mr.

Nelson [the principal] to put your name in the logbook, and for that, you are not going to come out to anything good in life.") What she was saying was that because my name was recorded in the principal's logbook, my academic and professional career was over. Not having the full understanding of what it meant to have your name recorded in a logbook, I took my foster mother's remarks literally. I felt hopeless to the point that I did not want to go back to school anymore.

However, those two incidents taught me a valuable lesson because I never participated in any more childish acts or pranks, no matter how tempting they were. I do believe that after having gone through all the female shoes drama, in which I had been shunned and humiliated, I probably was trying very hard to fit in with my peers. Perhaps if I had been forced to wear another pair of female shoes, I would not have gotten myself into so much trouble throughout my fourth-grade year.[5]

Stringent Cost-saving Measures

Now that I have described my foster parents' abusive behavior, I will provide you with a synopsis of their stringent cost-saving measures as they related to the foster children. I know that you would like to know how my first school year ended and what happened to the pair of female shoes. Well, several months later, I ceased wearing the pair of female shoes because one of the heels broke

---

5 I would like to point out that I was the only foster child who had participated in childish activities while at school. The fear that our foster mother instilled in us was well known and was enough to keep the foster children in check.

off. Would you believe that my foster mother got angry because she thought that I had deliberately snapped the heel off because I refused to wear the shoes anymore? Regardless of the outcome, I had to attend school barefooted for several months. That was also humiliating! It was like "jumping out of the frying pan into the fire."

I was relieved when my foster mother bought me my first sneakers. Although they were two to three sizes bigger than my actual foot size and I was forced to fill the unoccupied space with lots of newspaper, it was a hallelujah moment for me. I was happy knowing that I no longer had to go to school barefooted or be seen wearing a pair of female shoes. I can still remember the pair of Bata sneakers I received, and how they gave me the impression that they were built to last. Unfortunately, the pair of Bata sneakers fell apart within a couple of months, and once again, I had no other choice but to attend school barefooted. My brother found himself in the same predicament. Would you believe that our foster mother claimed that we were the ones who had deliberately destroyed the sneakers so that we could get new ones? She did not view it as natural wear and tear. It did not matter if our sneakers were used or abused, because George and I had to attend school barefooted throughout the times we had no shoes, which was most of the times. Not only that, but there were times when we had to go to school barefooted for the entire school year. Not to mention the fact that we had to work in the maggot-infested pigpens and chicken coops barefooted as well.

We also had what I would describe as a "brief" problem. In this context, I mean underwear. There were times when George and I had only one pair of underwear each. Whenever we come home from church or school, we had to wash it and hope that it dried (not by electricity or gas, but by solar and wind) by the following day. For the many years that we spent living with our foster parents, we received only one toothbrush each. We used them until there were absolutely no more bristles left on them to brush our teeth. I wish we had floss because we spent a lot of time picking the bristles from between our teeth.

While I am on this toothbrush episode, I might as well fill you in on another "need to brush my teeth" episode. One Sunday morning, long after my only toothbrush had fallen apart and after not brushing my teeth for a while, I remember one of the church brothers, whom everyone addressed as Pupa, came over and sat beside me. Not only was he sitting a little too close to me, but he compounded his problem by initiating a brotherly conversation. However, after exchanging a few words of "hello, how are you, happy to meet you" salutations, he turned to me and asked, "Do you have a toothbrush?" I told him I did not, and he assured me that he would provide me with one. Sure enough, the following Sunday, he came over to where I was sitting, sat beside me, and discreetly took a toothbrush from his jacket pocket and gave it to me. At the time, I was wondering why he had to be so discreet because I was delighted to have a new toothbrush. However, with what I know now, I believe he was a bit concerned about how my foster parents would react if they found out that he was giving me things. In hindsight, I should have asked Pupa if he had forgotten the toothpaste, the mouthwash, and the dental floss. Okay, such a request would have been overly presumptuous, but it wouldn't have hurt to have asked for a little toothpaste.

These were just a few of the many cost-saving measures my foster parents imposed on the foster children in their care. To be clear, I do not want my conversation in this or any regard to be interpreted as my brother, and I was ungrateful. We were fully aware of this because the clothes we were wearing were the only attire we had brought with us from the orphanage. Moreover, we were grateful for the clothing and other necessities our foster parents provided us irrespective of the quantity, shapes, sizes, or the frequency at which we received them.

Now that I have provided you with a precursor of what was to come, I will take you back to the sequence of events that occurred shortly after my brother and I commenced living with our foster parents.

CHAPTER 3

THE UNRAVELLING

Barry's Untimely Departure

Within several weeks of our arrival, the "good days" at home were numbered and the atmosphere became even more stressful. My foster mother adopted a zero-tolerance policy for any form of behavior that she deemed unacceptable. It all started with Barry. I could hear the argument going back and forth, and it became quite clear that something was definitely wrong. Based on my understanding, I believe that Barry was resisting our foster parents' more so our foster mother's unfair treatment. However, what Barry did not realize at the time was that my brother and I were his replacements. Although my understanding of what was going on was quite murky, I knew enough to conclude that Barry's days at the house were numbered. I got up one morning and saw Barry packing his clothes into a suitcase. That was when it became clear that Barry was being removed from the house. Later that morning, my foster father returned Barry to his family in St. Mary. Barry's final goodbye was the last time I saw and heard from him.

....

87

My heart goes out to Barry because he was never given the opportunity to excel beyond the ninth grade or even to acquire a proper vocational skill. This was a calculated decision by my foster parents because their sole intention was to extract as much free labor from Barry with little or no regard for his academic or career advancement. I remember on several occasions when Barry would go out of his way (implicitly and explicitly) to let my foster parents know that he would like to have joined the army (Jamaica Defense Force). To prove that he had a yearning desire to do so, Barry would purchase and wear green army-looking attire, fantasizing about being a soldier. However, instead of allowing him to fulfill his dream, they denied him such opportunity. In addition to the farm chores, Barry had to work at a little home-based, makeshift candy operation because my foster parents never gave him an allowance, which was the same for the foster children. (As for the candy operation, Michael, George, and I missed Barry even more because we had been the beneficiaries of a few tasty candies that he would bring home for us.)

After Barry's departure, my foster mother ratcheted up her aggression toward my brother and me to a completely new level. All of our chores had to be completed in the allotted time and to her satisfaction, regardless. This aggression was not just about the chores, but also with the ownership of things as it relates to her adopted son, Michael. One Sunday afternoon George and I got a real powerhouse beating from our foster mother for playing with Michael's toy. Even to this very day, I can still remember the black and gold, futuristic, zero-defect, engineered-to-precision, toy minivan Michael had received for his Christmas present. Whenever he was not around, my brother and I could not resist the temptation. Okay, enough with my drooling over this futuristic toy. The real question is why we would go out of our way to play with Michael's toys and risk being punished in such a manner.

Before you go off speculating, here is the truth and nothing but the truth. For the entire time, my brother and I spent with our foster parents, we were never given a single Christmas present. Our foster mother told us that we were not deserving of anything. She even told the church pastor not to provide us any Christmas presents. Every year, especially around the Christmas season, the pastor would purchase some of the most delicious chocolate bars from the Highgate chocolate factory for the children. However, my foster mother would let him know that he should not give George or me any of the chocolate. That is, everyone else was entitled to chocolate except us. However, when our foster mother was inside the house, the pastor would come to the backyard where my brother and I were and give each of us one whole chocolate and told us to eat right away.

Just by witnessing his subtle actions, I can assure you that the pastor did not approve of our foster mother's behavior in such regard. In fact, he told us that when he asked her why we were not deserving of any of the chocolate, she could not provide a fair response other than that we were not entitled to receive anything. In fact, her actual remarks were, "George and Desmond don't deserve to get anything!" She did not have the same assertion regarding her adopted children. She bought toys for her adopted son but, as for us, we got none.

So, as it related to not having any toys, George and I had two choices, either to do without or to play with

Michael's toys and run the risk of being punished. On that particular Sunday afternoon, we chose the latter. However, Michael saw us playing with his toys and went hollering to his mother. He was crying so hard one would have thought that George and I had taken all his toys away from him and given him a beating too. Regardless of what happened, my foster mother intervened and gave us a severe beating. This beating could be classified as the Guinness World Record for the worst beating ever. With each blow she delivered, she echoed one of her unforgettable remarks, "Unnu cum yah com seem, an unnu nah run im fram yah." ("You guys came here and saw him, and you are not going to chase him away from here.")

After enduring that severe beating, my brother and I decided that we were not going to take any more of our foster mother's abuse. We had made up our minds that we were running away from home for good. With that said, we took off down the street. However, after running with no sense of direction or destination, we decided to stop and think things over. After conversing for a while, we realized that running away from home was not such a good idea. So we went home. If we had the means to go back to the orphanage, then we would undoubtedly have been there in a heartbeat. However, we did learn two valuable lessons. First, never set out on a journey unless we were absolutely sure where we were going and to whom. Second, never assume that Michael's toys are for everyone! In hindsight, whenever we saw Michael's toys lying around unattended, we should have echoed Admiral Ackbar's popular quote, "It's a trap!" Okay, you will have to wave the Google magic wand to uncover this one.

Narrowly Escaping the Colossal Bangarang

Here is another reason why my foster mother's home had become a very stressful and frightening environment for us. I remember one Saturday morning my foster father came home from work and went directly to the refrigerator and poured out a little of the condensed milk that belonged to one of the girls who was boarding with the family. Would you believe that my foster parents turned such a small misunderstanding into one of the most contentious arguments I have ever heard? Not only that, but it also led to other severe, unintended consequences. After a long and drawn out, back-and-forth argument, my foster father got into a rage and turned over the elegant dining room table causing two of the legs to snap like matchsticks. (As for George and me, there was no need for us to worry as long as our little wooden bench on the back verandah remained intact.)

Sadly enough, the bangarang did not stop there. He then tossed all the flowerpots from the verandah ledge and continued knocking over other things that were within his reach. And just as I thought the drama was over, I heard him say, "A guh drive di van thrue di house an mashup di wola it." ("I am going to drive the minivan through the house and smash it to pieces.") I thought he was bluffing or, in the words of a Jamaican, "A joke im a joke man." ("He is joking or just kidding.")

But he really got our attention when he got into the minivan, started up the engine, and revved it a couple of times. I was not sure about the others, but I found myself bracing for a colossal bangarang. However, instead of seeing the minivan come crashing through the house, I saw it go backward out of the garage and onto the road at a high rate of speed. I am not sure if he had changed his mind at the last minute or if his natural instinct had taken over and caused him to put the vehicle in reverse instead of drive. Whatever the situation was, he drove away and didn't return until the following day. Another similar incident occurred, but this time it had nothing to do with milk but over a couple fritters that my foster father claimed had not been cooked properly. Not only that but this contentious argument cost us a beach trip that I had been looking forward to for a long time. In hindsight, I should have intervened and asked if I could have the fritters because apparently my foster parents were not hungry. Ok, smile and move on.

Wow! How could small incidents such as pouring a little milk from the wrong container and a couple of undercooked fritters could have transformed into such a terrifying outcome? These were not the only frightening events, but I believe these two are sufficient to make my point. After having gone through a detailed analysis, I found out that the milk and fritters incidents were only the spark that lit the fuse in an already volatile relationship. Therefore, I would like to propose that all families implement a form of "relationship control valve." This way we could ease the psychological pressure that tends to build up over time. Yes! I know relationships are not that simple. However, if you can come up with a more human-like approach, then please feel free to make a note of it in the space provided below.

____

____

____

EXTENDING THE FAMILY

One evening, out of nowhere and with no prior warning, our foster mother showed up with a little girl, who was approximately seven or eight years old. She told us that her name was Carmena and that she would be living with the family. To be brief, she was another foster child. The real question is why my foster parents would go out of their way to foster another child when they already had four.

Nonetheless, it did not take long for Carmena to adjust to her new life and her new chores of helping to keep the house and the yard squeaky clean. She was placed in the first grade at the Stewart Town All-Age School. Although I did not know her past, it was apparent that initially she was quite happy to be living with her new foster family. However, her happiness was cut short because, within a couple of weeks, she became the recipient of my foster mother's harsh treatment. Her life became even more complicated after her welcome with my foster parents was terminated abruptly. Most likely, she was dropped off at the CDA or returned to the orphanage. So what could have warranted such a swift removal of this little girl from their house after just a couple of months? It was not as if she had been causing any trouble at home or at school. She was willing to work and abide by my foster mother's rules and her harsh boot-camp study sessions.

The day before Carmena was removed from the house, I heard rumors that one of the students had reported to my foster mother that Carmena had been seen exiting the male restroom with one of the boys. In hindsight, I do believe that the child who reported the incident did so in a way that gave my foster mother the wrong impression. With no hesitation whatsoever, my foster mother rained down her wrath on Carmena, without taking into account that this was an orphan child who was approximately seven or eight years old and, most of all, was unable to read or write. Therefore, it would be highly probable that she could have wandered off into the wrong restroom if she had not been accompanied by any of her peers or schoolmates. Not only that, but while I was at the orphanage, the girls and the boys shared one restroom. There was no gender separation with regards to bathroom facilities.

At the time, and even to this day, I am still wondering why a simple misunderstanding could have led to such an enormous consequence! Why did my foster mother execute her "one strike and you are out" policy against this little girl? After this incident, I did not see or hear from Carmena again. Therefore, I was unable to find out from her what really happened. I just cannot imagine how heartbroken it must have been for Carmena. I firmly believe that my foster parents, more so my foster mother, were more concerned about their self-proclaimed righteousness and prestige rather than the well-being of this innocent child.

By the way, I was six months shy of my eleventh birthday, was unable to read or write, and was taken from an orphanage where male and female shared one restroom. Therefore, I was quite fortunate that I had not gone wandering off into a female restroom by accident. Hmmm, I wonder if wearing a pair of female shoes meant that I was qualified to use the female restroom. Just a thought, nothing for you to think about. Well, in fact, some thirteen years later this very thing happened to me. Not because I was unable to read or write, but because I was simply not paying close attention. The point I am conveying is that anyone is prone to a few embarrassing mistakes at times.

THE RETURN OF THE FOSTER CHILD

One day a young man sort of magically appeared in the family. Other than his name, which was Roy, and the fact that he would be living with the family, we were not privy to any of the specifics. However, later I found out that Roy was my foster parents' first foster child, who had spent many of his childhood years being fostered by them. According to Roy, after living with my foster parents for a while, they, more so my foster mother, started to mistreat him, thus causing him to speak out against their unfair treatment. Instead of changing or modifying her behavior, my foster mother would punish and humiliate him even more. Unable to convince her otherwise, he decided that it would be best for him to leave their home for good, which he eventually did.

Several years later, my foster parents bought a minivan and arranged for Roy to operate it as a taxi. Roy was also permitted to move back in with the family. After living with the family for a couple of months, his strained relationship with my foster parents began to deteriorate. At the time, I did not have a full understanding of what the problem was, however, I remember it involved money and the use of the vehicle. Knowing my foster parents, I am quite sure that their expected returns on investment must have been grossly overstated. That is, they were expecting a lot more money than Roy was actually bringing in. In fact, I overheard my foster mother telling her husband that she had been told by several people that the minivan was always filled with passengers and, based on that, Roy should be bringing in more money. Anyway, after enduring a number of my foster parents' accusations and nagging complaints, Roy decided that he was no longer going to work for or live with them. Not only that, but Roy was not pleased with the unfair treatment that George and I, especially my brother, were subjected to. With that said, he packed his bags and left.

Most likely, Roy had thought that his former foster parents, especially his former foster mother, had changed. However, he found out the hard way that they were still the same people. Their extreme love for money and their deceptive behaviors had not changed.

ARRIVALS AND DEPARTURES

Adding Three Johnsons to the Family

Shortly after Carmena's departure, my foster parents took in three teenage children (Maxwell, Ann, and Carol Johnson) to board with the family. Ann was the eldest, followed by Maxwell and then Carol. Why would my foster parents assume the additional responsibly to care for three more children? Okay, let me not beat around the bush, because this arrangement was based solely on its economic value. Knowing the type of person my foster mother was, it caused me to wonder why Mrs. Johnson would want to entrust the safety and well-being of her children to her. Approximately thirty-two years later I had the opportunity to speak with Mrs. Johnson, and she told me that she had met my foster mother at a teacher's conference and she had appeared to be a very nice person. With that in mind, she entrusted her children to the care of my foster parents while she was away in the United States of America.

Unfortunately, Mrs. Johnson was not alone in this regard. In fact, Geroge and I had been led to believe that our prospective foster parents were wonderful, loving, and caring people, based on what the CDA representative had told us. Also, our initial experience gave us the impression that we would be living in the land of utopia. However, we found out quite early that we had been grossly misled in such regard. Mrs. Johnson and her children experienced the same rude awakening. My foster mother exemplified the true nature of the scripture that states that the outward appearance of a person can be quite deceiving. Just below the surface of what we perceived to be honesty and trustworthiness were the unseen characteristics of lies and deception. This experience is a lesson for all of us, including systems, and nations to learn from. We must examine ourselves thoroughly to ensure that we do not find ourselves deceiving and betraying the trust of others, especially the less fortunate children!

With the new addition, we had what I would describe as a full house. There were now three girls and four boys living under the jurisdiction of my foster parents. With that many children under one roof, it is now time to find out how the next set of events unfolded. As for the living arrangements, Maxwell shared a room with George and me, while Ann and Carol shared one room. Ann and Carol attended St. Hilda's and the Westwood (girls' only) High Schools, respectively. Maxwell attended the Stewart Town All-Age School with the rest of the family, except for Joy, who also attended Westwood High School.

Let's Just Add One More Person to the Family

Shortly after the Johnsons' arrival, my foster parents leased a grocery store and took in one of their family members to operate it. One Saturday afternoon, my foster parents brought a young man, Phillip, into the home and introduced him to the rest of the family. What was even more surprising was when they told us that Phillip would be living with the family and would be operating their grocery store. In retrospect, I would say that he appeared to be in his mid-twenties. Once again, this was another decision that had been made purely for financial gain. This arrangement meant more money for my foster parents, which meant that it should have been a win-win arrangement for everyone. Okay, not so fast. It turned out that this decision added a lot more friction to the already stressful environment we called home.

Wow! With the addition of this young man, there were now ten people, including my foster parents, living under one roof. To accommodate Phillip, my foster mother needed to lighten up the boys' room a bit. With that in mind, I was told to share another room with her adopted children Michael and Joy. For a while, my foster parents' home started to look and feel like a mini orphanage.

Other than that minor disruption, everything was going fine. Not only that, but the grocery store was also heaven-sent for all of the children because whenever we were feeling hungry, we could always count on Phillip to provide us with snacks. The snacks turned out to be a good complement to the fruits we used to harvest from the property across the street. I'm not sure why, when given a choice between fruits and sweets, children always choose sweets and snacks over fruits and vegetables. The only catch is that we had to run approximately three miles to and from the shop, which turned out to be a good calorie burner for the sugary snacks we were consuming. Okay, so far so good.

Phillip's Departure

Please forget about the "so far so good" I alluded to earlier because the house of cards was about to come tumbling down. And it surely did when we heard a shocking revelation that Joy was pregnant. With five boys in the house, the real question was who was responsible? And in the words of DJ Shaggy, "It wasn't me." It did not take long before our foster mother found out that Phillip was the responsible party. This incident created a whole heap of bangarang inside the home. One morning I was jolted out of my sleep by a massive commotion. I ran into the dining room to see what was going on, and that was when I saw my foster mother pounding away on the table with her fist while Phillip was trying to eat his breakfast. She was pounding her fist on the table so hard that it caused most of Phillip's scrambled eggs to slide right off his plate. Who knows, probably the constant pounding on the table was the reason why Phillip's over-easy eggs got transformed into scrambled eggs. The heated rhetoric ended that morning with my foster father removing Phillip from their home. This incident definitely placed everyone in a panic mode. Sometimes I felt like screaming, "Why can't we all get along!?"

At the time, I had no idea what was really going on or why my foster mother was so upset with Phillip. Moreover, in my own minute understanding regarding life, I just could not see what Phillip had to do with Joy's choosing to have a baby. Looking back, the foster children incurred a great loss because Phillip's departure meant that we could no longer receive our regular assortments of snacks. Also, Joy was removed from the home for the rest of her pregnancy.

This whole incident could have been prevented if my foster parents' decisions had not been driven by their extreme love for money. They were the ones who had created the environment, but their actions gave the impression that they were not about to accept any of the responsibility. Instead, they unleashed their anger at the individuals who needed their support in such a critical time.

Nonetheless, the doom and gloom that overshadowed the home were replaced with good news when Joy gave birth to a baby boy, Christopher, and returned home. From my point of view, this baby was not just another addition to the family, but more of a blessing that was brought into the home and one that had a positive influence on not just me but also my foster parents. I will explain my rationale later.

Now that Christopher had joined the family, our foster mother hired Sister Lin, a church member, to take care of the baby. Sister Lin was a live-in helper, which meant that she arrived on Sunday and departed on Friday. However, Sister Lin's babysitting and helper role ended shortly after Jacqueline's arrival. (I will provide details regarding Jacqueline shortly.) Although I did not know the exact reason for Sister Lin's departure, one thing I know for sure is that it was not easy to please my foster mother and she was always reluctant to make any decision that would cause her to incur a financial cost. I really missed Sister Lin because she was always a happy, jovial person. She fostered a wonderful relationship with the children. We always look forward to her Sunday afternoon arrival because we would receive a slice or two of her tasty potato puddings. Without any prejudice, I can genuinely say that Sister Lin baked the best sweet potato puddings I ever had.

Let's Make Room for One More Foster Child

Shortly before Sister Lin's departure, my foster mother knew that she needed a helper. However, instead of hiring a helper or a babysitter, she decided to foster another child. Who was this child and where did she come from? Her name was Jacqueline, and from the little I was told, she was a teenage girl who was residing at one of the orphanages. Although at the time I was unable to grasp the real meaning of fostering, I can assure you that my foster mother took Jacqueline from the orphanage not out of love and compassion but because she needed someone to do the household chores and assume the babysitting responsibilities.

The real question that I ponder over is why the CDA allowed my foster parents such latitude? Why were they allowed to "foster" a child at will? Was it because of their status, their influence, their worldly possessions? Or was it because of what they professed to be that no one, not even the CDA, dared to question their motives? Was their prestige so convincing that all they had to do was simply ask and a child was given unto them? Or was it because they were able to hide their injustice behind a justifiable cause? From the outside, their actions appeared to be noble but, deep in their hearts, they harbored other selfish desires.

As for Jacqueline, there was no such thing as a "good time" transition period. She was assigned most of the household chores right away. Seeing that Jacqueline was now tasked with the household chores and the babysitting duties, my foster mother got rid of Sister Lin. My foster mother would resort to extreme measures to have her house spotless. In fact, "Cleanliness is godliness!" was one of her favorite phrases. I can recall several occasions when she would rub her fingers across the top of the furniture and the hidden, hard-to-reach places, and woe unto us if her fingers picked up any dust residue. For me to explain what my foster mother really meant by her cleanliness/godliness facade, I will share with you one of my personal experiences of how she conducted her cleanliness policy.

In one instance, I was given the task of dusting the furniture throughout the house. However, my understanding was, "If I cannot reach it, then I cannot dust it." With that in mind, I dusted and cleaned everywhere on the furniture except the out-of-reach places. After I had been at this task for a while, my foster mother decided to conduct a thorough dust inspection. She started out by sweeping her fingers across the top of the furniture and, sure enough, her fingers accumulated quite a bit of dust. In other words, I failed the dust inspection. She repeated the process several times and then wiped the dust all over my face as if she were giving me a face painting. After she was through giving me a facial makeover and the dust has settled, she told me to go and dust every piece of furniture including the hard-to-reach places throughout the house. Thank God, I had only received a mild punishment—that is, having dust being wiped all over my face—rather than having to endure a physical beating.

My foster mother would conduct spot checks to make sure that the entire floor throughout the house had a mirror-like shine. If it were not so, then we would be told to buff the floor a second or third time. This reminds me of the frequently used "do until" computer programming logic. That is, we should keep buffing away at the floor until the desired mirror-like shine is met. There is a lot more, but I hope you get the point that my foster mother's desire was to have her house squeaky clean at all times.

The Abrupt Departure of the Johnsons

After a while, my foster mother started to exhibit a much harsher demeanor toward the Johnsons. At the time, I was not sure what the real issue was, however, the little that I knew was more than enough for me to conclude that the Johnsons' days at the house were numbered. Based on what I know today, the harsh treatment of the Johnsons started when my foster mother determined (according to her break-even analysis) that the car that Mrs. Johnson had bartered as the initial payment of her children's room and board accommodation had run out. This was sort of a barter trade in which the car was used to cover the room and board expenses for a period and then Mrs. Johnson would commence payment thereafter. Anyway, knowing the type of people my foster parents were, I believe they had no intention of incurring any costs beyond the break-even point.

She resorted to keeping a tab of every dime she had to spend, including the Johnsons' meal portion size. In fact, one of my foster mother's most irresponsible behaviors was on full display when Ann asked her for a piece of the chicken breast. That day, my foster mother gave Ann a verbal scolding that sent a barrage of shockwaves throughout the entire house. She let Ann know that, in her house, the chicken breasts were reserved for her and her husband and that Ann should eat what was given to her.

George and I were outside on the back verandah when this incident occurred. However, we heard every word because our foster mother was yelling at Ann as if Ann had violated her most sacred rule. I simply could not believe that a person could be scolding a child because the child had asked for a piece of chicken breast! Not the whole breast! Only a piece! My foster mother's anger would have caused anyone to speculate that Ann had made a formal request for a whole chicken. Seeing that my brother and I were the ones taking care of the chickens, we probably should have requested a piece of the chicken breast to replace the little scraps we were getting. Can you imagine what would have happened if George or I had made such a bold request? Our foster mother would surely have reintroduced us to our father's ital dish.

Shortly after that, I witnessed another incident that led me to conclude that the Johnsons' days at the house were indeed over. One evening I came home from school and saw Maxwell crying. I noticed that one of his hands was swollen to the point that I thought that he had gotten stung by the legion of wasps that were hiving in the backyard.[6] My assumption turned out not to be the case. Instead, it was my foster mother who had used one of her lethal leather straps to beat Maxwell because he accidentally broke a child's ruler.

---

6 The backyard was filled with lots of bananas, plantains, and sugar cane that had become "Home Sweet Home" for the legion of wasps that resided in the backyard. I mean, everywhere you looked there were wasp nests. Not only that, but many of the nests were hidden discreetly beneath the leaves. Whenever hunger set in, we would risk being stung just to get a sugar cane, a couple of fingers of ripe banana, or a plantain. To fend off the wasps, I would submerge myself in a large crocus bag, but even then, one or two of the wasps would find their way into the bag and sting me while I was attempting to harvest a tasty treat.

However, it was the next encounter that provided me with a glimpse into my foster mother's cold and calculating mind. While Maxwell was in the kitchen in tears, explaining the incident to his sister, my foster mother barged into the kitchen not to apologize, but instead to reprimand Maxwell. She said, "Yes, man! Yuh a behave like yuh a di man inna di house! A hope yuh tell her dat a yuh put yuh han inna di way." ("Yes, man! You are behaving as if you are the man inside here! I hope you let her know that you are the one who put your hand in the way.") The minute I heard my foster mother's remark, a deep sense of anguish resonated through my mind that is quite difficult for me to explain even to this day. She was blaming Maxwell because he had used his hand to shield the blows from his body! Was she not thinking about what she was saying!? At the time, I thought that there had to be more to the story than Maxwell had told us. However, his version of what had taken place was verified because the abuse had occurred in his classroom in the presence of his fellow classmates, including his teacher. Maxwell's classmates were also upset to have witnessed the abuse that he had suffered at the hand of the very person who had been entrusted to care for him.

Although I did not know much about parenting, I knew that the aftermath of what I was witnessing had nothing to do with punishing a child but, instead, was an outright abuse of a child. Throughout the writing of this chapter, I tried really hard to rationalize my foster mother's behavior as it may or may not have related to her past. However, in Maxwell's case and many other instances, I found it quite difficult to justify her actions. How is it that a person who professed to be of sound mind could inflict so much pain and suffering unto a child for something as simple as unintentionally breaking a ruler? The only possible conclusion I could draw from this incident was the fact that my foster mother got into a rage because Maxwell's action had caused her to incur a financial cost. One thing I had learned quite early is that there was a heavy price to pay when our actions or inactions caused my foster parents to incur an unintended financial cost. Also, can you imagine that Maxwell's abuse was considered the norm as it pertained to the foster children, more so my brother? If Maxwell was not beaten in such a manner most likely he would not have known that such a beating device exists.

Shortly after that incident, Mrs. Johnson took her children away from my foster parents' home. Although I missed them, I was quite happy for them because they no longer had to put up with my foster parents' abuse. I am quite sure that my foster parents would have treated the Johnsons differently had their mother provided them with lots of money. From that point forward, I never saw or heard from the Johnsons until approximately thirty years later. I have explained the details of this wonderful reunion in volume 4 of my autobiography.

The foster children were also victims of my foster parents' greed. I believe that monetary greed was one of the reasons, if not the main reason, why George and I had to walk to and from school barefooted and had to work on the farm barefooted as well. In addition to the open wounds, we suffered from a foot fungus known as ground itch. Jamaicans label this foot fungus as grunitch. This fungus rotted the flesh between our toes. The most gruesome of times was when we had to remove the pig feces and the accumulated compost from the pigpens and chicken coops.

This compost was the byproduct of wood dust and feces. Whenever we used the shovel to remove the compost, it exposed the "gazillions" of maggots that were beneath the surface. From that point, we would have maggots crawling all over our feet. Not only that, but the compost would produce heat that we could sense beneath our feet. It also emitted a stifling odor that, at times, would become unbearable. After George and I were through working in the maggot-infested pigpens and chicken coops, we had to use the force of the water from a garden hose to rid our feet of maggots and feces. This whole experience is still fresh in my mind even to this very day.

Our suffering was a twofold situation. That is, due to our many open wounds, we were unable to concentrate while at school. In fact, while in class, we could not keep our feet still due to the flies (known to Jamaicans as jinji flies) that would feast on the fluid that was oozing from our open wounds. Those flies were persistent! We simply could not get rid of them because the classrooms were opened to the outside. We would resort to just about anything to soothe our wounds. In addition to Band-Aids, we would use Benjamin's Healing Oil and Ajax as wound care. As for the Band-Aids, we could not replace them fast enough before they were once again saturated with the fluid that was oozing from our open wounds.

There were times when we would have no other choice but to sneak away from home (for which we would be punished) and go to the local clinic to have our wounds dressed. I remember the nurse would get really upset with us. She would say, "Lawd Jeezas! Bwoy! A weh mek unnu hab summuch sore pan unnu foot!" ("Lord Jesus! Why do you boys have so many sores on your feet?") The nurse on duty really had her work cut out for her whenever George and I showed up at the clinic. Forget about treating each wound, the nurse would drench our feet with a purple ointment that would have us looking like the Avatars. Whenever a concerned person inquired of our foster mother why we had so many open wounds on our feet, she would respond by saying, "A bad dem bad." ("They are bad children.") Even to this very day, I am still trying to understand my former foster mother's rationale. What is the correlation between being a bad person and having open wounds?

Why Ajax and Healing Oil as a form of wound care? Concerning the Healing Oil, I am not sure. Probably the word healing was what caught our attention. However, I did some brief research and found out that it should not be used on open wounds because it was meant to be used as a rubbing ointment for the relief of minor aches and pains. It just dawned on me that we could have applied this product to our bodies after receiving one of our foster mother's severe beatings. Well, it would not have worked because the label clearly states that it is effective for *minor* aches and pains, not for *major* aches and pains. And come to think of it, we spent our lunch money and the little proceeds we made from selling homemade cricket gears (balls and bats) on this product for nothing! I think we deserve a full refund.

As for the Ajax, this is based on an incident that I would like to share with you. This incident took place while I was at the famous Dunn's River Falls in Ocho Rios. There I was having a good time, climbing the falls for the very first time. Approximately halfway up the falls, I fell into one of the deeper water pockets, and within a couple of seconds, I found myself gasping for air. Immediately a tourist gentleman came to my rescue and snatched me out of the water. He immediately noticed that I had many open wounds all over my feet and in a concerned, caring, and informative manner, he told me that the river water was not good for my open wounds. My question is whether this tourist was really concerned about my open wounds or was he more concerned that I was contaminating the millions of gallons of water flowing down on his comrades below? Anyway, one argument led to the next, and he told me that I could apply Ajax to my open wounds. Being desperate and having no knowledge of first aid or wound care, I did accordingly. Not only that, but my foster parents had more than enough Ajax, due to the many pots and pans that my brother and I had to wash each day. In hindsight, I should have said, "Ha, Mr. Tourist Guy, if you think my open wounds are cause for concern, then please take a look at my brother's feet." I don't think he would have recommended Ajax; I believe he would have immediately notified the authorities.

Throughout the writing of this chapter, I decided to investigate the reason why this tourist gentleman would have recommended Ajax. I took an Ajax and a Comet (same product, different brand) container and read the labels carefully. I did not find anything regarding wound care. However, the first two words that jumped right out at me were "disinfect and cleanse." My first reaction was, wow! That was exactly what our open wounds needed. After reading the label, I also found out that it is a violation of federal law to use the product in a manner inconsistent with its labeling. With that said, I would like you to please keep this between us because I do not want the Feds to know that I violated the use of this product.

The most alarming aspect of this incident was the fact that a total stranger, who was from hundreds if not thousands of miles away, could have immediately noticed that it was not normal for a child to have that many open wounds! While, to the contrary, my foster parents pretended as though it were nothing to be concerned about! In fact, what this total stranger had witnessed was well known to my foster parents and their allies but, unlike the total stranger, they chose not to care and turned a blind eye to those (the children, in this instance) being harmed in the process.

I also wonder why the church members who were present did not have the same alarming concerns that this gentleman had. Most likely, my foster parents' actions in this, and many other regards, were overlooked because of their significance to the church, which was not worth sacrificing or losing no matter the cost being borne by the innocent children. The action of this total stranger exemplified the parable concerning the good Samaritan, of whom Jesus spoke, asking us to do likewise (Biblical reference).

I have used a graphic depiction to illustrate the physical suffering that my brother and I endured throughout our childhood. This affliction was entirely preventable, had it not been for our foster parents' extreme love of money and their total disregard for the well-being of the children who were placed in their care. This outright abuse was even more disturbing because my foster parents resorted to child-labor practices as a way to enrich themselves. Their only concern was to exploit the lives of innocent children to amass wealth.

Foster Children Academic Progress

Now I will fill you in on my first and only attempt at the high school Common Entrance Exam. Throughout my primary school years (1979–1982), the Common Entrance Exam (no longer available today) provided students who were enrolled in the fifth and sixth grades the opportunity to pursue the high school track.[7] Please see Appendix C for a brief overview of the Jamaican Academic system.

I am not sure why my foster mother provided me with this opportunity, because just a couple of months prior she had told me that I would never come to anything good in life. Not to mention my foster parents' love of money and their desire to have it all. With that in mind, one could see why this decision came as a big surprise to me. Regardless of the reason, I regarded this opportunity as something extraordinary because the depressed feeling of knowing that my life was over had finally ended. Not only that, but this was a way for me to redeem myself from the unfortunate fourth-grade incidents I discussed earlier.

Come to think of it, I would not be surprised if the costs had been financed by the CDA and not my foster parents. Nonetheless, on the first day of class, the teacher, Mrs. Nelson, presented me with a list of the required textbooks and workbooks. However, my foster mother refused to purchase the required textbooks and workbooks I needed when I presented her with the list. She only paid

---

7 Resources regarding the more recent education system can be found at the following sites: http://www.moe.gov.jm/, https://www.cxc.org/, http://www.classbase.com/Countries/Jamaica/Education-System, http://www.heart-nta.org/. Also, for a comparison of the United States' education system, please visit https://www.ed.gov/.

for the tuition and bought me a notebook. This was a clear indication that I should find someone willing to share his or her books with me. However, it was quite difficult for me to find someone willing to do just that. Although I did not have the required books, I did not let that stop me from showing up to class. After showing up to class and not having the required books, Mrs. Nelson asked one of the students to share her books with me.

Ladies and gentlemen, sit back and enjoy the show because this is where the "I wish it were not so" inconvenience episode begins. I can never forget this little girl who was forced to share her books with me. She wore a pair of glasses with very thick lenses (the Coca-Cola bottle type), and her hair resembled that of little Goldilocks. Not only that, but she had to hold the book at an angle for her to focus. And just like little Goldilocks, she never stopped turning the book until the angle was just right. For me to get a glimpse at her book, I had to position my head at the opposite angle. Today I can treat this as one big comical event, but at the time, nothing about this decision was funny as it related to this "poor" little girl. And let me emphasize, she was quite upset with me!

Not only that, but she was also the Speedy Gonzales of test taking, and there I was holding her back with my snail-paced learning. She would answer all ten or more questions on the current page before I could get through with the first three or four. She would then turn the page on me without any prior warning. And when I lifted up the page just enough so that I could peek under it, she would slam down her hand on the book and say, "Yuh fi mek yuh mumma guh buy yuh book!" ("Let your mother buy you your own book!") She was absolutely right for many reasons. Hmmm, I wonder if she would have granted me a little more empathy if I had been wearing a pair of female shoes? Just a thought.

Not having the textbooks and workbooks meant that I was not able to successfully complete any of the required classwork and assignments. The year went by rather quickly, and it was time for me to sit the Common Entrance Exam. After looking over the first couple of questions, I realized that I needed another two years' worth of classes just to understand the instructions. I had zero confidence because I was too nervous, way too slow, and at times lacking the desired reading and comprehension skills. After I was through with the exam, I knew right then and there that my hopes and dreams of attending high school were in jeopardy. And so I envisioned it, so was it manifested. When the results were published, my name was nowhere to be found on the successful candidates' list. Neither was the girl who had been forced to share her books with me. I believe to this very day that I am the reason why this innocent girl failed the exam. For the entire school year, she was forced to share her books with me.

Although I had not witnessed it, I believe she must have passed the exam the second time because I was not around to be a nuisance to her anymore. That was it for my high school dreams because my foster mother never gave me a second chance. I can assure you that this incident caused me much psychological pain because I had been really looking forward to attending high school!

I was the only foster child who was allowed to pursue the high school track. Neither Jacqueline nor my brother was given such an opportunity. Although George was more advanced academically, however, due to his outspokenness, my foster mother cared for him the least. In fact, I witnessed many occasions when my brother would try to get a little attention from our foster mother by saying, "Mam, we tek care a all di animals dem." ("Mam, we are through taking care of the animals.") Instead of showing a bit of appreciation, she would shout at him by saying, "George! And what do you want!" In hindsight, this would have been a good time for my brother to start listing a couple of tangibles and intangibles, such as I need love, compassion, a pair of protective shoes, and more. Nonetheless, my brother would reply by saying, "Nothing, mam," then he would walk away in a very depressed manner.[8]

It was obvious that my brother was only looking forward to a "Thank You! Great Job!" or some other token of appreciation. Instead, he was quickly put down. In other words, our foster mother displayed utter contempt toward my brother. It was George and me who had to toil day after day to take care of the chickens and livestock, but our hard work was overlooked and often discredited. For the entire time that we were living with our foster parents, we never received any appreciation for our hard work. Not even as much as simple Thank You! Instead, we were addressed as dogs, scavengers, and told that we were not deserving of anything. In fact, on several occasions we were told specifically that we would never come to anything good in life. However, George was the one

---

8 Just to be clear, when we used the word mam, it did not signify mother but was, instead, a gesture of respect, similar to Ms., Miss, or Mrs. Actually, we were specifically told not to address her as mom, mummy, mommy, or any other label that could give the impression that she was our mother.

who received the daily barrage of insults, humiliations, and beatings. Our foster mother even went as far as to let him know that he was going to live and die like a dog.

Throughout one of my conversations with the Johnsons, some thirty years later, they reminded me of the barrage of humiliation and physical abuse that had been directed toward my brother and me by our foster parents. They also stated that, at one point, my foster father got really upset with his wife and told her to stop abusing George. The most important takeaway from this conversation was when they told me that this was the first time that they had witnessed George smile and display a glimmer of happiness. However, despite my foster father's speaking out on that day, he did very little and in many cases contributed to the abuse of the children. Not only that but his intervention only made matters worse for my brother. My foster mother would punish him a lot worse whenever her husband was not around. In fact, I overheard heard her punishing my brother while saying, "Yes man, Coltie nuh deh-yah fi tek up fi yuh now." (Yes man, Coltie is not here to take up for you now.") It was not until the writing of my autobiography that I was able to come to terms with the severe forms of punishment and the daily barrage of insults and humiliations that were levied at the foster children, especially my brother.

My foster mother never cared about my academic career after the fifth grade. The same went for the other foster children, including Jacqueline and George. We were left to fend for ourselves academically. Our academic life was further complicated when Jacqueline, George, and I were transferred from the fifth grade to the seventh grade. Why the seventh and not the sixth? I do not have a definitive answer and can only speculate as to why we were forced to skip a grade. First, we were outstanding academic scholars and proved worthy of being in the seventh grade. Second, by not having access to copies of our birth certificates, it could be that we appeared to be much older than our peers. Third and final, it might have been another cost-saving measure enacted by our foster parents, in which they needed to rush us through school so that we would be available to work full time taking care of the farms and the other chores. Okay, let's forget the speculation of the foster children being outstanding academic scholars, because that would require setting the academic bar to a new low. Regardless of the reason, this was a very bad decision because it meant that we had to forego a whole year's worth of academic fundamentals. As for me, I found myself with an even steeper learning curve. I guess I should have known that there would be some form of consequence for failing the Common Entrance Exam. Despite the setbacks, we were very fortunate to have completed our end-of-year exams successfully, which meant that our foster mother did not have to incur any additional costs.

More Money, More Work

Shortly after the departure of the Johnsons, my foster parents significantly increased the number of chickens, pigs, and goats they had on the farms. They also took on a contract to supply one of the major hotels with fresh fruits and vegetables. Therefore, in addition to our regular chores, my brother and I had to accompany our foster father to several orange plantations to harvest oranges. Not only that, but I was tasked with selling the surplus fruits and vegetables at the open farmers market located in Clarks Town, Trelawny. It was as if they were in a hurry to make up for the lost revenue caused by the closure of the grocery store and the departure of the Johnsons.

One of our most dreaded tasks was to transport many bags of animal feed; not with a vehicle, but on our heads. I can assure you that it was not an easy task walking barefooted while carrying fifty pounds of animal feed on our heads! This we were forced to do even though our foster parents had two motor vehicles! I cannot forget the very first time I set out on this journey; everything was fine for the first quarter of a mile. However, what was first considered to be just another manual task started to feel like a severe burden. That is, after the first quarter of a mile, the fifty-pound bag of feed felt as though it were sixty pounds. After another couple of hundred feet, it felt as though it were eighty pounds, then a hundred pounds, and so on and so forth. Even though I alternated the load among my head, shoulders, knees, and toes, by the time I reached home, the fifty-pound bag felt as though it were a thousand pounds. (Please ignore the knees and toes portion of my comment above; I simply could not resist the hook of the popular children's song.)

Transporting the animal feed without the aid of a vehicle did not last for long because George built a handcart that we used to transport the heavy loads among the different farms. Although having a handcart was essential to alleviating the enormous burden we were subjected to, our foster parents refused to provide us with the materials to build the cart. In fact, my brother's requests in this and every other regard were always denied. However, George refused to give up. His mentality was, "Where there's a will, there's always a way." With that said, he pleaded our case to Mr. Chen, our neighbor, and Mr. Campbell. They both stepped in and gave us the supplies we needed. Mr. Chen provided us with the bearings that we used to make the wheels, while Mr. Campbell, the owner and operator of a lumber yard, provided us with the lumber. Once again, my brother was the chief architect for the handcart project. Before I proceed, I would like to extend my sincere thanks and gratitude to Mr. Chen and Mr. Campbell for reaching out to us in this regard.

As I pondered over this experience, I found myself asking what could have caused Mr. Chen and Mr. Campbell to have heard the fervent plea of a child and act accordingly, while my foster parents, who had heard the exact same plea, chose to do nothing. How could it be that these two strangers could be so generous when they were not the beneficiaries and had nothing to gain from the outcome? Once again, I know you have realized by now that my foster parents' sole intention was to acquire everything at the expense of others, even to the point that they would impose unnecessary burdens on the foster children.

RESISTING THE UNACCEPTABLE

After a while, the overwhelming amount of work and the unjust treatment caused my brother to become resentful toward our foster parents. This further complicated the fragile relationship he had with them, more so our foster mother. I remember one evening my foster mother gave my brother a severe beating. I am not sure what the reason was. However, from what I can recall, my brother was always reminding our foster mother that we deserved to be treated better and that she should refrain from addressing us as dogs and scavengers. His outspokenness seemed to have irritated our foster mother's ego and in return, she unleashed some of the severest forms of punishment on him.

On many occasions, she would strike my brother in his face and insult him in the most derogatory manner. In return, my brother would try to explain, saying, "But mam, why?" She would interrupt him, saying, "George, don't but me before I have to bax [slap] all your teeth down your throat!" How she slapped us (more so my brother) on our cheeks made me realize that she was not just speaking figuratively. To justify her actions, she would accuse my brother of being rude and ill-mannered. However, I came to realize that my brother was never rude or ill-mannered. Instead, he was only speaking out against injustice. In return he was humiliated and physically abused.

Here is one incident to highlight this point even further. While living with my foster parents, I suffered from an awful stomach pain that plagued me for approximately three years. Many days this stomach pain was so severe that I would find myself hunched over with water-like fluid gushing out of my mouth. It felt as though my stomach was continually being pierced by many sharp objects. The pain would cycle every ten to fifteen minutes and continue in that manner for several hours. Even to this day, it is still quite painful for me to explain what was really going on inside my stomach. In Jamaica, we labeled this symptom "burn stomach." The medical terminology is acid reflux or heartburn.

Despite my constant complaints, my foster mother did not regard it as urgent or a situation that warranted any medical attention. In fact, George and I suffered from severe ailments such as heartburn, fever, headache, mumps, toothaches, boils, ear infections, infected open wounds, and foot fungus, especially between our toes. However, from our foster parents' perspective, none of those conditions justified a trip to the doctor or the clinic. Neither did they take the necessary steps to prevent these ailments from occurring and recurring.

As for the heartburn, I cannot forget one particular day when I felt an intense pain radiating throughout my stomach. It was so severe I felt as though I were about to die. Now I know why this symptom is labeled heartburn, because on that day, even my heart felt as though it were on fire. The heartburn was so painful that I was unable to stand or sit upright. After observing me for a while, my brother had seen enough and decided that he was going to take action instead of just standing there and watching me suffer. With that said, he ran into the dining room where my foster parents were and told them that I was outside spitting up blood and that I needed to go to the doctor right away. Immediately after that, my foster mother beckoned me to come to her. She asked me what the matter was, and I told her that I was experiencing severe stomach pain. My foster parents determined that I needed to see a doctor the following day.

However, this episode took a wild turn when my brother informed me that he had told our foster parents that I was spitting up blood instead of clear liquid. I do not remember the exact conversation we had, but I remember informing my brother that our foster parents were really worried and that we needed to let them know that I was spitting up clear liquid, not blood. With that said, we went into the dining room together, and I explained to our foster parents that it was not blood that was coming out of my mouth. My brother tried to explain further, but our foster mother turned to her husband and said, "Coltie, yuh si how George an Desmond wicked. Dem yah a two wicked bwoy." ("Coltie, George and Desmond are two wicked boys.") Then she chased us both out of the house. Not only were we chased out of the house, but we had to stay out of her sight for many days.

I am not sure if my brother really thought that I was spitting up blood, but being a child and not weighing the consequences, my brother was only concerned about my well-being. Moreover, he had witnessed my suffering many times before due to this horrific heartburn. I believe that George knew that if he simply had told our foster parents that I was suffering from heartburn, most likely that would not have provided them with a sense of urgency or garnered their full attention. My brother's level of frustration could be attributed to the fact that our foster mother was always directing a barrage of dismissive insults and connotations toward us. I believe that our foster parents were quite upset because my brother would have caused them to incur a financial cost that they deemed unwarranted. With that said, I had to live with that severe heartburn untreated for more than three years.

There were only two instances in which I remember receiving any form of basic first aid care from my foster parents. The first was when my foster mother applied ointment to a boil that had ruptured at my groin and hindered my mobility. And even then, she complained every time she had to apply the ointment to my wound. Although she did not mention it, I do believe that she was most upset because I had caused her to incur a financial cost and the fact that throughout such time, I was unable to do my chores. Her, second act of goodwill happened one day while I was running a very high fever, to the point that I felt as though I were about to breathe my last breath. That was when my foster mother decided to intervene, apply Vicks vapor rub to my body, and give me a cup of a hot alcoholic beverage (Dragon Stout), which she told me to drink and then go to bed. From what I can recall, my brother and Jacqueline never received any medical attention whatsoever. George never, at any time, received any first aid, no matter how severe his conditions were.

There were at least two instances when my brother let our foster mother know that he was not going to take care of the farm animals and chickens unless she changed her attitude toward us. My brother exact words were, "Mam, mi nah guh feed yuh chicken an yuh goat an yuh pig, yuh watch." ("Mam, I am not going to take care of your chickens, goats, and pigs until . . . , you will see). Instead of changing her attitude toward us, she would respond, "Okay George, yuh du dat, an see if yuh get any food fi eat." ("Okay George, you do that and see if you get any food to eat.") Sure enough, after two or three days of not taking care of the animals and not getting any food to eat, my brother had to give in because he realized that he was holding onto a losing proposition. Throughout such times, she would not allow me to eat outside because she did not want me to share my meals with my brother. Although I was told to sit inside the dining room, I had to sit on the floor behind a cabinet because my brother and I were not welcome to sit with the rest of the family at the dining table. Sitting on the floor was nothing new, because George and I had gotten used to the idea of being classified as dogs and being told to sit on the floor. As for the pigs, goats, and chickens, they had their regular meals because I had to pick up the workload. In hindsight, this is the time I should have been in solidarity with my brother, but once again, I was more concerned with not losing the basic necessities that my foster parents were providing us.

George would also try to justify the need for us to wear protective shoes or waterproof boots while working on the farm, especially while cleaning the pigpens and the chicken coops. However, our foster mother would interpret my brother's plea differently. She would get very angry and respond with one of her usual phrases, "George! Did yuh bring any inside here?" In this instance, she was letting my brother know that he was welcome to protective shoes only if he had brought them with him from the orphanage. I am not sure what she meant by that. It was not the responsibility of the CDA to have known that my brother and I would need protective shoes before transferring us to our foster parents' care. The CDA representative could not have known that my brother and I would be subjected to such inhumane conditions!

My foster mother scoffed at my brother's pleas because she perceived him as having a sense of entitlement. At one point, she even had me thinking that my brother was asking for things that we were not entitled to. However, today, I can assure you that my brother was not asking for anything that our foster parents could not afford. Nor was he making any unjustifiable claims. Although I did not know the monetary value of a pair of protective shoes at the time, I am quite sure that my foster parents would not have sacrificed much.

THE ETERNAL, PHYSICAL, AND EMOTIONAL SEPARATION

Finally, my brother ran away from home because he could no longer tolerate our foster parents' physical and psychological abuse. I remember the day he came to me and said, "Mi bredda, com mek wi lef dis-yah stinking place." ("My brother, come let us leave this rotten place.") However, I decided not to go with my brother because I remembered how our first attempt at trying to run away from this very house had been unsuccessful because we had nowhere to go and no one to turn to for support. I asked George where we would go and to whom? Not in such an eloquent manner, but I did manage to get the point across. However, my brother was determined, and there was nothing that I could do or say that would cause him to change his mind. I was heartbroken and emotionally distraught as I stood there and watched my brother walk away from the house and the very people who had been entrusted to be the parents he never had.

The following morning when I woke up, I saw my foster mother busy taking care of the animals. By the way, she had on the necessary protective attire, including a pair of waterproof boots that covered her feet all the way to her knees. I could not help but wonder why she was not working in the maggot-infested environments barefooted but it was ok for George and me to work in such conditions barefooted? This is further proof that my foster parents knew that working in maggot-infested environments barefooted would definitely cause harm to a person.

As I looked on, my foster mother said to me in an angry tone, "Yuh si, wen yuh bredda show up, mi a guh tek im right back a di Child Development Agency!" ("You see when your brother shows up, I am going to take him right back to the CDA.") She continued by letting me know that I did not have to stay and that I could go and join my brother. Her actual words were, "Yuh caa guh jine im, yuh nuh haffi stay." ("You can go with your brother; you do not have stay here.") I did not respond to any of her remarks; instead I intervened and assisted her with the chores. In this instance, I was implying that I was not going anywhere. On the one hand, my brother was doing everything possible to transform our foster parents' abusive system while, on the other hand, I was doing everything possible to conform to such a system. Although it may have seemed natural that I conform to my foster parent's rules, I found out later that conforming to injustice will never bring about change; it only prolongs the inevitable.

After having been away for almost a week, my brother finally decided to come back home. The minute he came home, he was summoned by our foster mother to take a shower, get dressed, and go and have a seat inside the vehicle. She said, "George, yuh tink yuh a di man in yah. My husband Coltie is di only man in ya." ("George, so you think you are the man inside here. My husband Coltie is the only man inside here.") My brother did accordingly, but was a bit reluctant to go inside the vehicle. However, my foster mother intervened and ordered him to get inside the vehicle and told him that he was no longer welcome at her home. Although I was unable to understand the magnitude of my brother's psychological trauma, it felt as though I could hear my brother's voice deep within his soul, crying out for someone to help him. All I could do was to stand there and watch as my foster parents drove away with my brother. And that was when I realized what had really happened. The very thought that I would never see my brother again was devastating! After having been together all our lives, it was very difficult for me to accept the fact that we were now separated.

Of all the things that were said and done that day, the words that my foster mother uttered concerning my brother were the ones that provided me with a window into her mind and the deep animosity she held toward George. Upon her return from dropping off my brother at the Copse juvenile correctional institution, in a very condescending manner, she said, "Yuh shudda si di look pan yuh bredda face when wi tek im a Copse. Im neva waah fi cum outta di van." ("You should have seen the look on your brother's face when we took him to Copse. He did not want to come out of the vehicle.") She also told me that the man who had escorted my brother inside the compound had asked him how he could have left such a wonderful family to come to such a deplorable place.[9] What my foster parents failed to realize is that the worker

---

9 The man who escorted my brother into the compound got one thing right when he stated that Copse was a deplorable place. This assertion was substantiated by many reports, one of which was titled "They beat us here," by Petre Williams from the *Jamaica Observer* (2005).

who escorted my brother into the compound had exemplified the very essence of the scripture, "Man looks on the outward appearance, but the Lord looks on the heart," (1 Samuel 16:7, ESV). In this situation, the man was assuming that the people who had dropped off my brother had to be wonderful foster parents, based on their status and material possessions.

After seeing how distraught I was, my foster mother looked directly at me and said, "You are better off without him." At that moment I recalled the many times when she would remind my brother that he would never come to anything good in life and that he would live and die like a dog. However, what I did not know was that she would go out of her way to substantiate her words with actions. My foster mother's remarks, especially those she uttered that day, were a clear indication that she had gotten her heart's desire. First, she employed the divide and conquer strategy so that I would not be influenced by my brother's actions. Second, she knew that taking my brother to a juvenile correctional institution would make it almost impossible for him to experience a "normal" life. I also hold my foster father accountable because he was directly involved with the actions that were taken on behalf of my brother.

As it was in my brother's situation, I came to realize that whenever a person speaks out against injustice and challenges the very core of insanity, then such an individual will most certainly find himself or herself going against the grain of what is considered "the norm." In these situations, the consequences are severe, and justice rarely prevails; and so it was in my brother's case.

It is quite difficult and painful for me to understand why my foster parents—who professed to be Christians, who spent much of their time in church pastoring and leading the choir, who spent much of their time reciting hymns and scripture verses, especially those pertaining to love and compassion—would do everything in their power to destroy a child's life and then relish the process. Was it because they were annoyed by my brother's relentless cries for justice? Was it because he would no longer be of any financial value to them? Throughout those dark and defining moments, there was no one there to hear my brother's cry. In the end, the desperate cry of an innocent child was not enough to change the hearts and minds of his oppressors. This was the final incident that defined my brother's destiny.

My foster parents' actions validated the concerns that my father had regarding those who professed Christianity. Based on what the CDA representative had told us, I am confident that my foster parents' religious personae had been taken into account throughout the adoption process. This ordeal reminds me how much easier it is for us to reach into the Bible for a verse of scripture or a song from our favorite hymnbook than it is for us to reach into our hearts for a deed that reflects love and compassion. As a listener for many years, I can assure you that the choir songs orchestrated by my foster mother and the messages preached by my foster father are indeed a true reflection of the compassionate gospel of our Lord and Savior, Jesus Christ. Unfortunately, the words of love and compassion that left their mouths never made it to their hearts.

CHAPTER 9

THE AFTERMATH

Despite my foster parents' doomed outlook concerning my brother, many days I found myself looking forward to his return. It was quite difficult for me to accept the fact that my brother was never coming back. There were times when I wished we had never been taken from the orphanage and placed in our foster parents' care. This is why it should not be a common practice just to remove a child from an orphanage and place the child in a home where there is a strong probability that the child could end up being abused. Removing a child from an orphanage should *not* be based on quotas, statistics, or convenience. Instead, it should be based solely on the recipients' desire to love and care for the child.

Adopted Children Sent off to Boarding School

Shortly after my brother's departure, my foster mother sent Michael and Joy off to a private boarding school. The house that was once buzzing with children had dwindled down to just Christopher (Joy's baby), Jacqueline, and me. The next visible change was when my foster parents significantly scaled back the number of chickens and animals

135

on the farm. This was because my brother's efforts were no longer available to them. However, despite the significant reduction in the number of farm animals, there was still quite a lot of work to be done. I was tasked with taking care of the remaining farm animals, maintaining the lawn and flower gardens, and operating a home-based grocery store. By the way, there was no such thing as a lawnmower or a weed whacker. Therefore, I had to use a machete to cut the lawn and weeds from the garden.

Jacqueline was tasked with cleaning the entire house and doing the laundry and, sometimes, the cooking. She was not allowed to use any of the electric appliances. Instead, she had to do the laundry by hand and get down on her knees and use a piece of cloth to polish the floor, then buff it with an old-fashioned coconut brush. This process is similar to waxing and buffing a car. In fact, none of us were allowed to use any of the electrical appliances. Before Jacqueline's arrival, my brother and I had been tasked with keeping the floor clean. We would spend several hours polishing and buffing the floor with a piece of cloth and a coconut brush. Now that Jacqueline and I were the only two foster children left at home, we would take turns babysitting Christopher in the evenings and when he was sick or there was no babysitter to take care of him.

Makeshift Grocery Store

I am not sure if operating a grocery store out of the house was the "bold" idea of my foster father, mother, or both. Regardless of whose idea it was, this was another moneymaking venture for my foster parents. Later I was summoned into what I would describe as a Retail Clerk 101 training session. The training session started out with a number of basic monetary calculations and "what if" scenarios. For example, my foster mother went over several simulations regarding the purchase of certain grocery items, the sum of such items, the total amount of money received, and the correct change due, if any. Even after that elaborate session, I still did not have any idea what my foster parents were up to. Could it be that they were planning on enrolling me in a prestigious business management school?

However, the reason became known when one Saturday morning, my foster mother told me to get dressed because I would be accompanying her to the wholesale supermarket. That morning I witnessed my foster mother on a grand shopping spree at Mr. Young's wholesale store in Brown's Town, St. Ann. She purchased several hundred pounds of rice, flour, sugar, cornmeal, salt, and many other grocery items. Although I was not exactly sure what the reason was for this shopping expedition, I was absolutely sure that she was not buying all that food for the household, unless she was planning on fostering all the children who were at Garland Hall. Better yet, was she about to operate her own orphanage? Okay, please pretend I did not raise those possibilities because we know what a disaster that would be. With all this extra food, I was really looking forward to a healthy increase in my portion size.

After my foster mother was through with her grand shopping, we went home. Later that afternoon, we transformed the garage into a makeshift grocery store and stocked it with the groceries. After we were through, my foster mother told me that operating the grocery store was now my responsibility. Then it finally dawned on me the reason why I had been subjected to such rigorous retail training. Well, none of the foster children were strangers to the buying and selling business venture. In fact, I was tasked with selling the surplus fruits and vegetables (leftover after supplying the hotel) at the open farmer's market, while, at the request of our foster mother, Jacqueline, George, and I had to sacrifice our school breaks and most of our lunch hours to sell candies, coconut cakes, and other snacks to our schoolmates. I can assure you that my foster parents would do just about anything to make a quick buck.

As it pertained to the grocery store, the regular business hours were Monday through Thursday, 4:00 p.m. to 8:00 p.m. I was no longer allowed to attend school on Fridays because the hours of operation were from 8:00 a.m. to 9:00 p.m. on Friday and Saturday. Monday through Thursday, I operated the grocery store out of the house, the dining room to be exact. Whenever a customer showed up at the front door, he or she would get our attention by shouting, "Hello!" "Serve!" "Youhoo!" (not Yahoo), or some other form of Jamaican attention-getting expression. Upon hearing one of those salutations, I would have to hurry to the front door and greet the person (similar to the Wal-Mart greeter but not as colorful) because he or she was not allowed inside the house. After greeting the customer and taking the order, I would go back to the dining room and gather all the requested items (fill the order). Then I would deliver the items to the customer, accept payment, and complete the transaction by providing the customer with the correct change, if any was due. Just to be clear, this was a cash-only operation. We did not accept cheques, debit, or credit cards; and certainly, no forms of e-pay either. Okay, there were no such things as debit, credit, or e-pay but you get the point that my foster parents operated a cash-only business. I presumed that my foster parents only accepted cash because they were fully aware of the "in God we trust" motto that is inscribed on the American currency. Not really, but who knows what was going on in their minds?

Friday and Saturday were the busiest and most tedious days with regard to the grocery store operation. On Friday, or occasionally Saturday, I would go to the wholesale market and purchase items such as rice, flour, sugar, salt, cornmeal, dried codfish (salt fish as per Jamaicans), and other produce. As soon as I got home, I would convert the garage into a makeshift grocery store and get ready for a long day of shop-keeping duty. I had to keep the shop open until approximately 9:00 p.m., or later if it was a holiday weekend. After ten to twelve hours of operation, I would return the groceries to the dining room. This moving back and forth of the groceries had to be done because the garage did not have the proper enclosure (no garage door).

As for the purchasing of the meat, my foster mother arranged with Ms. Duckworth, a grocery store owner, to have her purchase chicken parts (chicken backs as per Jamaicans) from the delivery truck and store them at her shop until I was able to retrieve them later that afternoon. On Thursday of each week, I would get up very early and get dressed for school as normal. However, instead of just walking to school, I would have to push a handcart approximately three miles to Ms. Duckworth's grocery store, located in Stewart Town. Upon arrival, I would leave the handcart, along with the money and the instructions with

Ms. Duckworth. I would then walk the remainder of the journey to school. In the afternoon, somewhere around 2:00 p.m., I would request an early dismissal (as instructed by my foster mother) and go by Ms. Duckworth's, where I would retrieve anywhere from two hundred to three hundred pounds (or it could be more, as per the demand) of chicken parts and transfer the boxes of meat to the handcart. Finally, I would "put my shoulder to the wheels" and push the loaded handcart three miles home.

In addition to transporting the chicken parts, I also had to transport several hundred pounds of animal feed, wood slabs, and wood dust to the different farms. This arrangement could have been a more manageable undertaking if my foster parents had used their vehicle to transport the groceries, animal feed, and materials. Neither did they want to incur the costs associated with chartering a vehicle.

Although I did not have a problem assuming the above responsibilities, I was very disturbed when I read my file twenty-seven years later and found out that my foster mother had written to the CDA complaining that she was not being paid enough to take care of me. Also, in other instances, she made direct requests for an increase in the stipend she was receiving from the CDA. She complained as if I had been a total liability to her. She made it appear as though the foster children had not contributed financially. My foster parents' constant demand for money was not exclusive to just the CDA. As a matter of fact, I happened to have a detailed conversation with Mrs. Johnson thirty-two years later, and she told me that my foster parents had written to her quite frequently, demanding more money. Although it was my foster mother who wrote the letters requesting more money from the CDA and Mrs. Johnson, I also hold my foster father accountable because their greed for money seemed to have no end.

As time went by, things started to deteriorate rapidly between my foster mother and Jacqueline. Jacqueline was being yelled at for not cooking the meals and cleaning the house to our foster parents' satisfaction. Even at one point, I heard my foster father raising his voice at Jacqueline, claiming that she added too much browning to the chicken. At that very moment, I should have reminded him that Jacqueline was taken from an orphanage, not a culinary school! I also witnessed Jacqueline being beaten many times for not cleaning the house to my foster mother's satisfaction. And let's not forget the little dust-up episode in which I outlined how my foster mother wiped her fingers across the top of the furniture and the hidden places, and then rubbed the accumulated dust all over my face. It appeared as though Jacqueline had found herself in the same predicament.

Remember the awkwardness of the grocery store setup and how Monday through Thursday I had to walk back and forth through the house to serve the customers? I will now share with you one of the episodes that led to other unintended consequences. On a very busy shopping day, there I was, serving the customers while leaving a trail of dust, grain, and meat trimmings all over the floor. I remember Jacqueline warned me on several occasions not to mess up the floor she was cleaning. However, I did not listen. Instead, I continued with my shopkeeper's duties as if I had not heard a single word Jacqueline had said.

Jacqueline had endured enough of my messing up the floor and, within the twinkling of an eye, the calm and peaceful girl I once knew suddenly transformed into a tiger.

And when I say tiger, I am not talking about Mr. Kellogg's "They are grrreat!" frosted flake tiger. Instead, I am talking about a fierce and vicious tiger. Before I could figure out what was happening, she leaped off the floor, grabbed me around my neck, latched her teeth into my arm, and gave me a very nasty bite. I would like to repeat a very popular African American phrase, "Girrrl, she ain't playing." She definitely got my attention and made me realize that something was wrong. Moreover, after seeing the blood and the teeth impression on my arm, I was fully aware that her action was a lot more painful than her spoken words.

Jacqueline told me that she was consistently being punished because she was not cleaning the house to our foster mother's satisfaction. I know that Jacqueline was speaking the truth because I had overheard my foster mother yelling at Jacqueline, letting her know that after she (Jacqueline) was through cleaning the floor, she (our foster mother) should be able to part her hair by looking at the floor.

From that point forward, I made sure that all my items were secured and that nothing ended up on the floor. Not only that but instead of walking across the floor, I would glide back and forth on a piece of cloth while serving the customers. This method solved two problems with a single solution. A little process I would like to coin as "serve and shine." That is, taking care of the customers while giving the floor the desired mirror-like effect. This incident would not have occurred if Jacqueline and I had been in school and *not* at home, cleaning and operating a grocery store.

In addition to our extra chores, Jacqueline and I had to wash and iron our clothes. When I use the words wash and iron, I am not talking about placing our clothes in a washing machine and simply turning the knob to the wash cycle or plug the clothes iron into the electrical outlet and *voilà*! all is done. Actually, we had to place our clothes into a washtub and scrub them clean with our hands. In fact, my foster mother would not let any of the foster children use her electrical appliances, which included the washing machine, electric iron, and electric floor polisher. I should say washing machines and floor polishers because she had two of each. Well, the spin cycle on one of the washing machines did not work properly, but who cares about the spin cycle when all we needed was the wash cycle. As for the clothes iron, we had to use the old-fashioned clothes iron that you placed on a charcoal stove or some other form of an open flame. I can assure you that one of the most daunting tasks for us was trying to gauge the temperature of those irons. Let me emphasize, there was no temperature gauge on those irons. We had to put our hands close enough to sense the heat being emitted by the iron.

While I am on this topic, here is a funny incident as it pertains to gauge-less clothes irons. Well, I should say funny now, because back then it turned out to be a costly blunder for me. Once upon a time, I took one of the clothes irons from the coal fire and placed it off to the side so that it could cool off a bit. I returned later with the assumption that it was now at the desired temperature, but found out that I was very wrong when I placed the iron on my polyester khaki shirt and witnessed an entire section, equal to that of the iron, went up in smoke. I do believe it was Jacqueline who took my iron that was at the optimal temperature and replaced it with one that was white hot. I was unable to press charges because I did not have a single shred of evidence to back up my claim. Okay, just smile because it was all my fault for assuming. Anyway, after this incident, I was left with one khaki shirt, which I had to wash and iron every other day.

I do believe that my foster mother did not care to have the foster children wash their clothes in the washing machine because we did not exhibit squeaky-clean hygiene. With regard to George and me, it was more obvious because we had to take care of the animals, and we had visible open wounds that were always oozing fluid. Jacqueline did not have any hygiene issues because she was not assigned to take care of the farm animals. However, she did have minor cuts and bruises caused by the severe beatings she received from our foster mother. Also, her feet were quite dry and flaky (ashy). However, her dry skin condition could have been easily remedied if only my foster mother had provided her with a little Vaseline Intensive Care Lotion. The point I am making is this: we had too many impurities and needed to be quarantined as much as possible.

Adding Two More Children to the Drama House

One day, out of the blue, two teenage girls sort of magically appeared in the house. Once again, my foster parents were getting ready to provide a one-year room and board accommodation for these two girls. My first reaction was, what happened to the parents of these girls? Hadn't they done their homework to know that the environment they were subjecting their children to was one I would not recommend? I wish there had been a rating system to allow parents to provide feedback regarding the level of care my foster parents provided their children. I could only imagine the barrage of negative feedback my foster parents would receive.

So who are these two teenage girls and why were they here? Deborah (Debbie) and Totlyn would be boarding with the family because they were students of the West-wood High School, which was located within proximity to my foster parents' home. I realize that this meant more money for my foster parents, but as for Jacqueline and me, it meant more work as well. However, to my surprise, the farm chores got much lighter shortly after that because my foster parents ceased rearing pigs and goats, and substantially reduced the number of chickens they reared. I am not sure of the reason, but it might have had something to do with money. Not having to take care of any pigs or goats, and only a limited number of chickens, was to my advantage because my open wounds had a chance to heal.

Totlyn and Debbie reminded me of my sisters Pauline and Paulette. At no time did their actions or spoken words make me feel like I was less of a person. They would go out of their way to ask me how I was doing. On several occasions, I wanted to let them know that Jacqueline and I were not happy living with our foster parents, but I chose not to because I was quite fearful of my foster parents. However, I did not have to say anything because the words and actions of my foster parents, more so my foster mother, were quite revealing and more than sufficient.

Totlyn and Debbie were quite jovial. Their presence brought joy into the home even though it lasted only for a short time. While I am on this joyful topic, I might as well share with you one of the funnier pranks that they played on me. I hope you will find it entertaining because I am quite sure it was entertaining for them too. I remember waking up one night only to find myself in the cold bathtub wondering how the heck I had got there. Although I am not able to recall all the things that were going on in my mind, I can assure you that there is a strong probability that I was thinking that it had something to do with my foster mother's exercising one of her improvised punishment methods on me. All my speculations were put to rest when, a couple of nights later, I caught Debbie and Totlyn red-handed trying to put me in the bathtub. Therefore, if you think the saying "Boys will be boys" does not apply to girls as well, then I am here to say think again. With these two girls, I would like to modify this phrase with no reservation to read, "Girls will always be girls."

Apart from the joy that Christopher, Totlyn, and Debbie brought into the home, life was getting quite complicated between Jacqueline and my foster mother. This tension reached its pinnacle one day when I overheard a loud commotion coming from inside the house. I had witnessed Jacqueline being beaten severely many times before; therefore, it was not uncommon to hear her crying and pleading to our foster mother to have mercy on her. In fact, it was quite terrifying and heartrending to see her on her knees pleading with our foster mother to stop hitting her. However, instead of heeding the plea of an innocent child, my foster mother would hit her even more forcefully while yelling, "Shut up yuh mouth!" Throughout such times, I felt like screaming at our foster mother, but it appeared as though I had lost my voice because of the extreme fear that had engulfed me.

Although my foster mother had two electric floor polishers (a Hoover and a Singer, to be precise) that Jacqueline could have used to give the floor its desired mirror-like sheen, she was not allowed to use either of them. Jacqueline's punishment was not exclusive to just physical beatings. On many occasions, she was not allowed to ride with our foster mother in the car either. She had to accompany my brother and me on the seven-mile journey to and from school each day. By the time she was halfway through the journey, she would be dripping wet with sweat. It was a heartrending experience to see her walking to and from school, while our foster mother drove by with a vehicle that had enough space to seat at least four more people comfortably.

Jacqueline's Departure

The following day after Jacqueline was severely beaten, I noticed that she was not at home. A couple of days later, my foster mother told me that Jacqueline had run away from home and gone back to the orphanage. She also informed me that Jacqueline had told the CDA many lies concerning her, one of which was that she had beaten her severely and produced visible marks all over her body. From what I heard, I firmly believed that the severe blows that my foster mother rendered unto Jacqueline that day would most likely have produced visible marks on her body. The physical abuse that was inflicted unto Jacqueline that day was not fitting for a wild beast much less a human being! Even to this day, I am still asking myself whether Jacqueline had been doing something that I was not aware of that would have caused our foster mother to inflict so much pain and suffering unto her? But knowing my foster mother, it did not take much for her to make a child's life miserable.

Being a recipient of her many forms of punishment, I know without a shred of doubt that her trademark was to inflict maximum pain and suffering by any means possible. The audacity of her to stand there with a straight face, trying to convince me that Jacqueline was not speaking the truth when my brother and I (mainly George) had been the recipients of her severest forms of punishment, and ones that left plenty of visible marks all over our bodies. Her collection of beating devices not only made our lives miserable, but they also produced plenty of visible marks.

I also witnessed what she did to Maxwell, who was not a foster child, but a boarder who had been entrusted to her care. With this much evidence, how could my foster mother expect me to believe that she had not abused Jacqueline! It is beyond human comprehension to imagine that my foster mother was trying to convince me, not a stranger, but a child who resided at the very same home and was subjected to the very same inhumane treatment that had caused Jacqueline to run away from home! Could it be that she had lost her mind? Or could be that insanity had become her norm? Her ability to think and act rationally was impaired because she valued material things far more than she did the lives and the well-being of the innocent children who had been placed in her care.

It was terrifying to witness, but even more heartbreaking to know that there was nothing that any of us could do. I can relate to the scripture, as it rightfully states, "Again I saw all the oppressions that are done under the sun. And behold, the tears of the oppressed, and they had no one to comfort them! On the side of their oppressors there was power, and there was no one to comfort them."

(Ecclesiastes 4:1, ESV). Even to this very day, I can still hear the cries of the innocent children who were being abused by my foster parents!

I cannot help but wonder, with this much writing on the wall, why the CDA did not realize that something was considerably wrong and the reasons why the foster children were running away from my foster parents' home. Moreover, in this instance, the evidence was clear because a child had visible marks as proof! And if those abrasions were not the result of a child's being beaten, then what else could they have been!? What more evidence did the CDA need to conclude that the children in my foster parents' care were being abused? If the presiding officers had done their due diligence, then they would have uncovered the truth. However, I do believe that my foster parents were given the benefit of the doubt because of their status, which included their acclaimed exceptionalism, economic, and religious personae.

On rare occasions, Mr. Wellington, the CDA officer, would visit the house, but we were too scared to let him know what was going on; neither did he ask. We realized that the CDA officer was only visiting for a short time, but it was we who had to live with our foster parents for a lifetime. Therefore, to avoid receiving a double dose of our foster mother's wrath, we learned to remain quiet and only answer with yes and no. I was scared to the point that I would hold my head down (staring at the floor) or looking off to the side to avoid making any eye contact with the CDA officer. That was when he would shout at me by saying, "Hold your head up, young man! You must hold your head up and look at the person who is speaking to you!" I would have done just that, but I could not do so with my foster mother standing there passing all sorts of remarks such as, "Yes man, yuh si im hold dung im head, like a snake in a grass . . ." ("Yes man, you see how he hung his head like a snake in the grass.") Mr. Wellington had no idea the clobbering we would receive if we made the mistake of making eye contact with our foster mother. In fact, she had explicitly told us not to look directly at her or stare directly at the face of an adult whenever such person was speaking, even if we were being addressed directly.

As for the very few times the CDA representatives visited my foster parents' home, I believe that they must have been ecstatic to have found us alive. Based on my experience, I would conclude that as long as they found the children alive, that seemed to have fulfilled their mandate. Whenever I reflect on this experience, it reminds me of the popular "It's alive!" phrase that was echoed by the mad scientist from the old Frankenstein movie. (Those of you who have no clue what I am talking about will have to go deep into your movie archives or simply Google it.)

On a more somber note, I would like to point out that allowing children to express their concerns was one of the more vital areas overlooked by the CDA representatives. Therefore, this was one of the important matters that I discussed with the presiding CDA officers during one of my visits in 2009. However, the representative assured me that allowing a child to express his or her concerns openly, or in private with one of the CDA representatives, is now being taken into consideration. The representative also stated that this practice is encouraged throughout the evaluation period. Knowing that a child's well-being is not left solely to his or her foster parents' discretion has brought a sense of closure in this regard. This is very personal to me because the foster children's fervent cry for justice was never heard.

Many years later, through an unfortunate situation, I was able to experience as a parent what a typical foster child, CDA process should have been for me as a child. Throughout this frightening ordeal, I also came one step closer to understanding what it was like for my biological parents when my siblings and I were removed from their care. See Appendix B for detail.

After Jacqueline's departure, I was the only foster child left at home. It was now just Christopher (Joy's baby), the two boarders, Debbie and Totlyn, and me. In addition to my daily workload, I was also assigned the responsibility of cleaning the entire house. My treatment did not improve simply because I was the only foster child left. Even though there were plenty of unoccupied chairs at the dining table, I still had to sit outside for all my meals because I was not allowed to sit at the dining table or on any of the chairs and couches. In fact, I was still being shunned and treated as an outcast.

Reflecting on how my foster parents treated the adopted children, I believe they must have known that their treatment toward the foster children was unjust. If it were not so, then they would have applied the same treatment to both sets of children, irrespective of the process by which they were assigned to their care. However, they employed a more just treatment as it relates to their adopted children when compared to the foster children. This blatant form of subjective parenting is a clear indication that they knew how to apply humane treatment to all the children. If we know in our hearts what is *fair*, what is *just*, and what is *right*, then we are not ignorant concerning justice without partiality.

Just when I thought my workload was easing, my foster parents went out and bought three calves and many beehives. Boy oh boy! They would do anything! And I mean anything possible to make a quick buck! It appeared as though financial maximization was their only life's philosophy. In this context, I believe they misinterpreted the real meaning of the phrase "cash cow." Or it could have been that they were attempting to have their home flowing with milk and honey. Irrespective of my added humor, this endeavor ended on a sad note when all three calves died within a couple of weeks. They died because my foster parents try to raise them on the cheap. Besides, I had no experience and not enough time to take care of them properly.

This sad episode started when my foster parents substituted powdered milk for the real cow's milk they had been purchasing from a local farmer. I was assigned the task of coming up with the right mixture for the calves. I had no idea what I was doing, and the three calves developed severe cases of diarrhea and died shortly after that. As for the bees, most of them ran away from home because my foster parents were working them too hard. Okay, that was not the reason. The reason was due to a lack of experience on our part.

While I am on this bee topic, I would like to share a little scary, "So Let It Bee" story with you. Well, what I am about to share is more of a confession rather than just a story. One day, while I was sitting down watching the bees going in and out of their hives, a little thought popped into my head. This little thought convinced me that it had been several weeks that these bees had been going in and out of the hives and there had to have been sweet honey inside the boxes by now. This temptation was overpowering because I was hungry. Not only that, but I could smell the sweet aroma of honey in the air. With that said, I took a cup and went to the beehive to fetch myself a cup of honey. Not having the slightest understanding of how the whole honey extraction process works, I went directly to one of the boxes and lifted up the cover. Instead of scooping out a cup full of honey, I found myself being attacked by many legions of bees. I quickly replaced the cover and ran away as fast as I could, but the bees kept coming after me. I fell on the ground, and for some unknown reason, I decided just to lie there and hope that the bees would eventually disperse. Luckily for me, that theory worked. The bees went back to the hive.

However, while I was there lying on the ground with the cup in my hand, Michael came by and inquired what was going on. Instead of telling him exactly what had happened, I somewhat jokingly told him that I had gotten a cup full of honey from one of the beehives. Before I could say another word, Michael took off running. I had no idea where he ran off to or why he was running in the first place. Before I could figure out what he was up to, I saw him running toward the beehives with a large cup. I tried to warn him, but it was too late. Instead of helping himself to a cup of honey, he began running away like a young, energetic calf, kicking and screaming with a swarm of bees chasing after him. He ran through the house, which prompted his mother to fend off the bees by dousing them with Baygon insecticide spray. That got rid of them, and he was spared.

I knew that Michael liked to eat, but I had no idea that he would really believe that it was that easy just to scoop out a cup of honey from a beehive. I guess he knew just as little as I did regarding the whole honey extraction process. Well, let's give him the benefit of the doubt, because he was away at boarding school when his parents brought home the beehives and issued a stern "Do not disturb!" warning. Although this incident turned out to be quite humorous, I felt very sad after discovering the seriousness of the situation. If it was any of the aggressive bees, we could have been hurt or killed in the process. I was relieved because Michael did not let his mother know that I was the one who had told him that there was honey in the box.

Adding a Helping Hand

As for the babysitting role, I had to stay home from school many days with Christopher because he was quite sickly. I was relieved when my foster mother hired Mrs. Dawson (one of the church members) to help with the babysitting duties and other household chores. Sister Dawson worked a regular 8:00 a.m. to 5:00 p.m. schedule. Besides, my foster mother allowed Mrs. Dawson to bring her baby, Dean, to work with her. However, this arrangement did not work out too well for Christopher because Dean, who was a couple of months older, would do everything possible to keep Christopher away from his mother. So what does that tell you? It is a clear indication that even a child understands that every parent must care for his or her own child. Unfortunately, such ideal conditions are not always feasible in today's society.

After observing what was taking place between Christopher and Dean, I found it quite sad and heartbreaking to leave Christopher at home. I had been babysitting him for a while, and we had developed a deep bond with each other. In fact, he used to address me as Bandon instead of Desmond. He would get up every morning and follow me around, holding onto my hand, or more like latching onto two or three of my fingers. On many occasions, when I was getting ready to leave for school, he would cry so hard that it would break my heart to leave him behind. With that said, on two occasions, I dressed him and took him to school with me even though it got me into a whole heap of trouble with my foster mother.

One morning I got up and noticed that Christopher was standing in my room, patiently waiting for me to wake up. That morning, he followed me around every step of the way while I completed my chores. Every move I made and every step I took, he was right there behind me. Just as I was getting ready to leave, he latched onto my hand very tightly. When I tried to wrestle my hand away from him, he started crying as if he were asking me why I was abandoning (or more like "Bandoning") him. I remember how sad and disappointing it was for me when my siblings and I were forcefully removed from our parents' care. And the times when my mother visited George and me at the orphanage and, instead of taking us home with her, she would walk away, leaving us behind. Not wanting Christopher to go through the same ordeal, and with no real thought of how I was going to take care of a three-year-old baby at school for the next seven to eight hours, I defied all logic and executed the "No Child Left Behind Act."

With that said, I dressed him, and off we went together to the bus stop. I remember while I was on the minibus the passengers were quite curious, inquiring of me where I was going with the baby and where his mother was. I am not sure what my response was, but what I do know is that I promised myself that I would never leave Christopher behind again. Now that I think about it, I wonder where I got the money to ride the bus instead of walking to school like I usually did? Most likely, it was my lunch money. Nonetheless, it would have been a daunting task walking approximately three and a half miles with a three-year-old child on my back.

Okay, let's forget about the money and the bus ride, because as soon as my foster mother noticed that I had brought Christopher to school with me, I could detect that she was quite perplexed. When she learned that I had taken the baby to school with me simply because he was crying, she got very angry with me. She said, "Lawd Jeezas, Desmond, a mad yuh mad! A weh you tek Christopher a school wid yuh fa!?" ("Lord Jesus, Desmond, are you insane! Why did you take Christopher to school with you?"). I tried to explain, but she did not want to hear any of what I had to say. Regardless of the reason, my foster mother had to keep Christopher for the next seven hours, and she was not happy.

One would think that I had learned my lesson from the first experience. No, sir! I simply did not. A couple of days later, I executed the "No Child Left Behind Act" once more.[10] Again, my heart was broken when Christo-

---

10 Okay, just so that you are not being misled, please browse this link, http://www2.ed.gov/policy/elsec/leg/esea02/107-110.pdf), for the true purpose for the No Child Left Behind Act (NCLB) of 2001.

pher held onto my hand and would not let go. Disregarding the overwhelming consequence that awaited me, I got him dressed and took him to school with me a second time. I must admit that it was not an easy decision, especially knowing that my foster mother would pour out her wrath on me.

Ladies and gentlemen, it happened just as I had envisioned it. My foster mother shouted at me in a very angry tone before the entire class. She said, "Bwoy, a mad puss piss you a drink or wat?" ("Boy, are you drinking insane cat urine?") Even to this day, I still do not understand what this phrase really means. Regardless, I was well aware of my foster mother's wrath. Not only did she threaten me with severe punishment, but she also demanded that I take Christopher home at once! I did learn my lesson because that was the last time I took the baby to school with me. However, morning after morning, it would break my heart when I had to wrestle my hand away from Christopher and walk away, leaving him behind crying.

I am still struggling to figure out what could have prompted me at such a young age to intervene on behalf of a child who was emotionally distraught, even though I knew the severe consequence that awaited me. Even to this very day, this experience is not an easy one for me to fully comprehend. However, I do believe that the emotional bond that Christopher and I shared was what stirred my heart to the point that I found it difficult to leave him behind. After careful examination, I realized that up to that point in my life, I had no real concept of what it is like to have experienced a motherly or a fatherly bond. However, a child who was approximately three years old was able to provide me with a life-changing experience that had never been manifested to me before.

Once again, my foster mother's helper arrangement did not last, because Mrs. Dawson left shortly after that. I am not sure why she left. However, I overheard my foster mother arguing and raising her voice at her on several occasions. I hope it did not have anything to do with taking Christopher to school with me. If so, then I do owe Mrs. Dawson an apology.

Now that Mrs. Dawson was no longer working for my foster parents, and Jacqueline was no longer around, my foster mother and I shared the babysitting duties. I had no idea how to take care of a baby, but I tried my best. Forget about the modern days' diapers and wipes. All I had to work with was nappies and a couple of safety pins. Whenever he made a baby accident, I would place him in the washtub and sort of hose him down. I used to enjoy cooking his favorite cornmeal porridge and chicken noodle soup. I must admit that I was eager to cook his meals because I used to eat some too. Even my foster father would help himself to some of the delicious baby soup.

As for the boarders, Debbie and Totlyn, they were now completing the final two or three months of their yearlong boarding with my foster parents. Other than the overwhelming workload, there was a silver lining because the house had gotten a bit quieter with respect to my foster parents' arguing and the constant crying of the foster children from being abused. Okay, let's not get too comfortable because there was much turbulence brewing on the horizon.

The Bandit

Here is the first turbulence that contributed to my worst financial nightmare. One busy Friday afternoon, business at the grocery store was booming and everything was going great! Well, the great feeling lasted only for a short while because, that day, I was robbed of every dollar I had in my possession. How did that happen? Okay, let me take a little time to refresh your memory. First, my foster parents had decided to operate an inconvenient grocery store out of their house. That is, the produce and other grocery supplies were physically stored inside the house. Hmmm, I wonder if they had gotten a permit for this. Most likely not! Anyway, Monday through Thursday, I operated the grocery store out of the dining room, and on Fridays and Saturdays out of the garage. On Fridays and Saturdays, I had to move the entire operation into the garage except for the meat and the other frozen produce, which were left behind in the dining room. And may I remind you that the dining room was not in visible proximity to the garage. On this particular Friday afternoon, there was a high turnout of customers, and everyone was doing extra shopping. I remember a man came into the yard and stood off to the side. I was not sure if he was there to shop or if he needed to discuss something with my foster parents or me. However, as soon as I was through with the other customers, he came up to the counter and presented me with a list. I served him all the items that were on the list except for the chicken parts.

Seeing that I had no one to watch the items that were in the garage, it meant that I had to leave everything behind unattended while I went inside the house to get the chicken parts from the freezer. The chicken parts were frozen solid, so it took me a while to get them loose. After I got the desired chicken parts and hurried back to the garage, I found that the man was gone. I mean, he was gone with the wind. I thought he had forgotten the chicken parts or he had to run a quick errand and would be right back. Anyway, whatever the decision was, I did not think much of it at the time. Moreover, the worst-case scenario was that I would end up not being paid for the groceries he had taken. It was not until the next customer came by and bought her weekly groceries before I realized that the entire day's take was missing. The man had stolen somewhere between $80 and $110, which was quite a lot of money in the 1983 fiscal period.

Many times, I thought about bringing this incident to my foster parents' attention, but I was very much afraid (more like terrified) to do so. I hope you had not forgotten how I explained in detail that we would suffer dire consequences when our actions or inactions caused my foster parents to incur a financial cost, or a financial loss as it was in this case. And let's not forget how my foster mother mistreated Mrs. Johnson's children because she claimed that she was not receiving the desired financial support. Can you imagine what would have happened to me in this situation?

Moreover, just a couple of months earlier, my foster father had given me a verbal scolding because I had let a passenger off the minivan without collecting his fare. And yes, including my regular chores, there were times throughout the holidays when I had to assume the conductor's role for my foster parents' minivan. One of my foster father's rules was that I should never let any of the passengers get off the vehicle unless I had collected their fares. That rule was broken one particular morning when a young man reached his destination and shouted the usual, "One stap, driva." I beckoned to him for his fare, however, he made it appear as though he was experiencing difficulty retrieving his money from his pocket. Not knowing what he was up to, I opened the door and allowed him to step out of the vehicle so that he could have unrestricted access to his pockets. The minute he exited the vehicle, he took off running down the road like a wild mongoose.

That was when it dawned on me that, instead of giving him unrestricted access to his pockets, I had given him unrestricted access to his feet. It turned out to be quite a spectacle for everyone when my foster father jumped out of the vehicle and started chasing after him. It got even more hilarious because he was unable to keep up with the young man. Not only that, but he exerted all that energy trying to recoup a fare that was only a couple of cents. I should have told my foster father to go ahead and deduct it from my allowance. Oops, you know I am only kidding because I did not receive any compensation for my conductor service either. That day I endured a barrage of verbal scolding from my foster father. It was so outrageous that even the passengers were not pleased with his behavior. They told him to give me a break because I could not have known that the passenger would run away instead of paying the fare.

Now that I have given you a glimpse into my foster parents' unmerciful, unforgiving nature concerning money, it is obvious why I decided not to inform them that a customer had walked into the shop, taken all the money, and walked right out undetected. Besides, I thought that there was enough time left in the weekend to generate enough sales to offset the loss. That hypothesis held true for a short while. However, within a couple of weeks, my foster mother discovered the shortfall. By then it was too late to let her know what really had happened. Knowing that my foster mother would never give me the benefit of the doubt so, I pretended not to hear her nagging complaints regarding her financial shortfall. However, I learned a valuable lesson that I should never leave money in the garage unattended again. Even to this very day, I still have an accurate description of the bandit, who was about five feet ten inches tall, light complexion, wearing a brown and white plaid shirt, and a pair of brown pants. Although it has been over three decades, do you think that the statute of limitations still applies? If so, then I need to go ahead and file a police report.

There were many things wrong with the way this grocery store was being managed. First, seeing that I was the only person operating the store, the goods should not have been divided between the garage and the dining room. Everything should have remained either in the dining room or in the garage. Second, the credit system that my foster parents adopted just to lure customers away from the other shops proved quite difficult for me to manage. For example, a number of the customers would make a down payment on what they owed while at the same time opening new lines of credit.

This financial system was similar to paying the minimum on your credit card while at the same time using it for other purchases. I would have arrows all over the logbook like pointers (computer terminology) trying to reconcile the differences. I wish I'd had an Excel spreadsheet because it would have been a whole lot easier to keep track of this convoluted credit system.

Third, we lost many customers due to my foster parent's unscrupulous behavior. The loss of customers is due to the fact that they were selling meat that was not fit for human consumption. What I am about to explain is a situation that has troubled me deeply even to this very day. One week my foster mother decided to purchase way more chicken parts than she normally does. Probably she got a deal that was too good to pass up. However, we did not have ample space in the freezer to store that much chicken parts, which meant that the fully thawed meat had to sit outside the freezer for more than 24 hours. As a result, the meet started to spoil. Not only that, but the exposed portion of the meat was also contaminated with maggots. Even though the evidence was overwhelming, my foster mother told me to put contaminated meat in the freezer when space becomes available. I knew right away that my foster mother did not want to incur the loss. As a matter of fact, the odor was quite high, so there is no way that she did not know that the meat was spoiled. I wanted to let her know that this was not right, but out of fear, I decided to do as I was told. The problem was compounded because the bad batch contaminated all of the meat that was in the freezer. Many of the customers returned the meat and others told me that they had to throw it out. Even when they brought it to my foster mother's attention, she was pretending as if the customers did not have a right to voice their legitimate concerns. Eventually, she was forced to discard the entire batch of meat. All this could have been avoided if my foster parents had done the right thing from the beginning and not let the love of money marred their conscience.

Last but not least, I should not have been at home operating a grocery store while I should have been in school!

Even before this incident, I overheard my foster mother on many occasions complaining that she had spent her entire teacher's salary in the business but could not see where the money was going. In other words, she was complaining that she had not received the expected return on her investment. However, as it relates to my foster parents, the ROI acronym should be rebranded as the need for them to *Root out Injustice* from their lives. In this context I am holding myself accountable as well because I should have stood up and let my foster parents know that under no circumstances will I sell contaminated meat to the customers! But once again, I chose to conform so that I would not lose the little provisions I was receiving from my foster parents.

I hope this is a solemn lesson for us, people, systems, and nations that it is not moral or ethical to condone with behaviors such as the ones exhibited by my foster parents. We should be mindful not to relinquish our moral obligations or undermine our conscience in our pursuit of monetary or material gain.

Being at the Wrong Place at the Wrong Time

Shortly after the theft incident, I found myself caught up in one of those "being at the wrong place at the wrong time" situations. It happened one day after I was through packing away the groceries from the garage back into the dining room. That evening I had a little too much time on my hands, so I decided to chitchat with Debbie. I am not sure what was so important about this conversation. Probably I was providing her with the bad news of how I had been robbed and how I was in need of a loan to cover the shortfall. I am quite certain that was not the topic being discussed, but I could not resist because it sounds rather fitting. Anyway, I remember she got up and said something to the effect of, "I am going home, so I need to finish my packing." It was a normal routine for the children boarding with my foster parents to go home to be with their family throughout the major holidays, including Easter break as it was in this case.

After Debbie was through packing, she and I started browsing through several magazines that she had found in her suitcase. I'm not sure why I was browsing through magazines when it was quite obvious that I could not afford to buy as much as a shoelace. Before I knew it, I fell asleep on her bed. Ooh no! Big mistake! There I was sleeping on Debbie's bed, having one of those "Life is good, no problem, man" sweet dreams. Okay, let's forget what I have just said concerning sweet dreams because I was about to experience the worst hell-on-earth nightmare.

Whenever Christophe woke up at night and in the morning, he would head straight to my room to make sure I was there. That particular night, he woke up, got out of bed, and went directly to my room, only to find out that I was not there. He started crying, which prompted my foster mother to go searching for him. My foster mother's frantic yelling was what frightened me out of my sleep. The minute I got up, I was hoping and praying that it was a dream, but unfortunately, that was not the case because I found myself on Debbie's bed and not in my room where I should have been. Surely, I was guilty of being in the wrong place.

After she was through yelling and screaming, I went to my room where I should have been in the first place. I went to bed, thinking that it was all just a minor misunderstanding, and the rest of the night would be my usual rest in peace (RIP) sleep. Yeah right! That was what I thought, but certainly not what my foster mother was thinking because she complained to her husband. Ladies and gentlemen from near and far, that night, I was jolted from my sleep by shock-and-awe blows that pounded every inch of my body. When I was able to gather myself, I found out that my foster father was lashing me with a lethal leather strap. The severe blows that were being unleashed on me were similar to a Roman soldier flogging a lowly peasant. My once sweet dreams were transformed into a raging inferno. I had no way of escaping the blows that were raining down on me. With every blow my foster father unleashed on me, he kept saying, "Desmond, yuh a no di man inna di house!" ("Desmond, you are not the man in this house!") I was not sure why he was flogging me, and why he was accusing me of trying to assume the "man of the house" title. And, just to be clear, not once have I ever professed verbally or in written form that I was the man of the house. I would definitely have been on a suicide mission if I had attempted to contest a three-hundred-pound person for the "man of the house" title. That night, only my face was spared, and that was because I tucked my face into the mattress for the duration. I could not believe that such a minor misunderstanding would cause my foster parents to get into such rage.

When it was all over, I had huge swollen marks and bruises all over my body as a vivid reminder never to make such a mistake again. From that point forward, I could only say hi and bye to Totlyn and Debbie from a distance. I regretted this silly decision on my part because it triggered several unintended consequences that went far beyond that day.

Shortly after the incident, Debbie and Totlyn left my foster parents' home and went to board at Westwood High School. It was quite apparent that they had not been happy boarding with my foster parents either. After their departure, it felt as though the house had become an uninhabitable place. Had it not been for Christopher, the house would have been one of the coldest and loneliest places on the earth.

Despite my added dramas, the psychological effect of this incident has become my most terrifying life experience and one that haunted my memory for a very long time. After witnessing what had happened to my brother and the other children, more so the foster children, I began to suffer from constant nightmares. This psychological effect (which I was not aware of at the time) was compounded exponentially when I was jolted from my sleep by the severe blows that my foster father rained down on me that night. I was terrified to the point that I found myself unable to sleep at night. I remember hearing footsteps coming toward me whenever I turned off the light and attempted to go to bed. At first, I thought it was Christopher coming to see me as he usually does. However, the footsteps I heard were undoubtedly not coming from a child but instead from an adult. Therefore, it caused me to wonder if it was my foster mother or foster father coming to my room to render another dose of beating on me. I must admit that I was even more scared because I should not have been sleeping on the bed that was in the room, but instead on the piece of foam on the floor.

There were many nights when I would turn on the light only to find out that there was no one there. However, as soon as I turned off the light and went back to bed, the same unexplainable phenomenon started all over again. It appeared as though the footsteps started in the dining room and continued into the passage and, finally, into my room. After getting out of the bed several times over several days but not seeing anyone, I concluded that it was either a ghost or my mind playing tricks on me. However, as I lay there, I could hear the footsteps getting louder and louder as if the person were coming directly toward me. Shortly after that, I felt as though a much heavier person was either sitting or lying on the opposite side of the bed, thus causing it to list or tilt. Seeing that I was on the opposite side, up against the wall, I felt as though I was pinned against the wall and unable to move. I wanted to get up and turn on the light but I could not because the only way for me to get to the light switch was to go across the side of the bed where the person (or what I perceived to be a person) was either sitting or lying. As I lay there on the bed, I started trembling and I would break out in a cold sweat. I would lie there for a while, waiting to see what would happen next. However, nothing happened. After lying there in a panic state, I would become exhausted and eventually fall asleep.

This went on every night! I became overwhelmed to the point that I would leave the light on until late in the morning. However, I did not want to fall asleep, fearing that my foster mother would get angry with me if she happened to come by and notice that I was sleeping with the light on. Not to mention that I was sleeping on the bed without her permission. I really thought that the house was haunted or plagued with ghosts. This strange phenomenon went on for many months. Hallelujah! This psychological trauma finally ended the day I was removed from my foster parents' home.

I found out thirty years later that what I was experiencing was extreme fear and that the side effects had nothing to do with ghosts, but instead, were due to the psychological state of my mind. Now it all makes sense why when I turned on the light, there was no one there! Stay tuned because this will become much clearer in volume 4, where I provide full details of another experience that resurrected my most traumatic childhood psychological fears.

THE OMEGA (Ω)

Applying My Brother's Rationale

After a while, I found out that no matter how much work I did and no matter how hard I tried to appease my foster parents, the less appreciative they would be. In return, I started applying my brother's rationale by speaking out against their unjust treatment. However, just like my brother, my actions in this regard did not go over well with my foster parents, more so my foster mother. Moreover, I failed to realize that I was on borrowed time and that asking for basic fairness was like pulling my last card from the deck. One evening after completing all my chores, I decided to socialize with the neighbor's children. According to my foster mother, I had not really completed my chores, because I should have been at home prepping the grocery store for the next day's operation. In other words, I should have been weighing out the rice, flour, sugar, salt, cornmeal, and other produce into different proportions.

After I was through socializing, I hurried home, somewhere around 7:00 p.m. As soon as I entered the verandah, I could hear the doors being slammed one after the other.

I thought my foster mother was closing the doors to keep out the insects and night creatures. Little did I realize that I was the insect and night creature that my foster mother was keeping out of her house. I tried to open the doors, but they were all shut and guarded like Fort Knox. I knocked on the doors, but my foster mother did not answer. I kept knocking on the door. Shortly thereafter, I heard the key turning in the door that is located between the verandah and the dining room. I was quite happy to know that my foster mother was about to let me into the house.

The minute she opened the door and I made the first step forward, I felt the most painful facial blows one could ever imagine. It was so severe that it caused my head to swing back and forth like a bobblehead doll. In the words of a Jamaican, "A one rawtid bax mi get inna mi face." ("She gave me a severe blow to my cheek.") It took almost three days before I could open and close my mouth without experiencing excruciating pain. In retrospect, instead of just talking with Mr. and Mrs. Lee's children, I should have been using the time to learn a few self-defense karate moves. If that had been the case, then I would have the intuition and the necessary skills to defend myself against my foster mother's ambush.

Despite my wittiness, the more pressing question that needs to be asked is this: What about my action could have caused my foster mother to display so much anger toward me? The answer became quite clear when I remembered that it was not too long ago that Mrs. Lee had confronted my foster mother regarding the manner in which I was being treated by her. Mrs. Lee had been trying to help my foster mother understand that although I was a foster child, that did not give her the right to treat me as any less than a human being. At first I thought that Mrs. Lee's intervention would cause my foster mother to examine her actions and change accordingly. However, instead of trying to understand the point Mrs. Lee was conveying, my foster mother got very angry with her and cursed her to her face. My foster mother told Mrs. Lee that it was none of her business and that she had the right to treat me in any manner that she deemed appropriate. In other words, I was her property, and she had the right to do whatever she chose with her property. After my foster mother was through reprimanding Mrs. Lee, she slammed the door so hard that it caused the entire house to shake. It also sent her elegant flower vase crashing on the floor.

Over the years, I had witnessed and had been the recipient of my foster mother's anger, but I was very much surprised at her behavior as it related to an adult. I had thought her anger and demeaning words were reserved only for the foster children. I was also quite surprised to know that Mrs. Lee would have taken the initiative to confront my foster mother, especially knowing that she did not care to be advised, questioned, or challenged regarding anything whatsoever.

Mrs. Lee had recently relocated to the community, but it did not take long for her to see the injustice that was being carried out by my foster parents. Being a person of sound mind and fair judgment, she was deeply concerned that I was being deprived of my human dignity. She realized that I was not being treated like a child but more like a servant. She noticed that I was forced to work on the farm barefooted, transporting hundreds of pounds of animal feed, building materials, and other grocery items for several miles with the aid of a hand cart, while my foster parents had two vehicles that they could have used for such purpose. She also noticed that many days I was not in school because I had to tend to the farm, operate a grocery store, and at the same time babysit a child. Mrs. Lee had seen and heard enough of the physical and psychological abuse and decided to intervene on my behalf. Unfortunately, my foster mother refused to acknowledge that her actions toward the foster children were unjust. Instead, she chose to unleash her anger at Mrs. Lee.

With that vivid recollection, I now understand why my foster mother was so angry when she saw me socializing with Mr. and Mrs. Lee's children. The injustice that Mrs. Lee was trying to confront individually should have been confronted collectively. Which is to say, what if the members of the church, the CDA representatives, the body of teachers, and the entire community had confronted my foster parents in the very manner Mrs. Lee had? Would that have made a difference? Would that have caused them to look deep into their souls and acknowledge that what they were doing was wrong?

The foster children were not the only ones who were crying out for help; my foster parents were also crying out as well, but unfortunately, no one could hear the cries of either person. As a community, as a body of believers, and as professionals, we need to ask ourselves how we could have failed my foster parents and the children by neglecting our responsibilities. Although there is no way of knowing at this time, I believe firmly that it would have been worth the effort if collectively, we had confronted my foster parents' injustice. A positive outcome would not only have been in the interest of the children, but also in the interest of my foster parents, the community, and humanity as a whole. Unfortunately, she was blinded by her superficial acclaimed exceptionalism, economic, and religious personae.

To my knowledge, Mrs. Lee was not a member of any church, nor did she profess Christianity, or associated with any other forms of the religious sect. In fact, the Christian community would have labeled her as an ungodly person and a nonbeliever. However, Mrs. Lee's action should remind us that if we just spend a little less time professing religion and a little more time confronting and challenging the evil deeds that are being perpetrated among us, then this world would be a much better place.

Seeking Refuge

One would think that after receiving that severe blow, my foster mother would at least have allowed me inside the house. But, once again, I was only dreaming. She slammed the door, turned the key to the lock position, and said, "Yes man, gu back weh yuh come fram!" ("Yes man, go back to where you came from!") I had no other choice but to sleep outside on the little wooden bench. That night, not even the dogs were pleased with me. They would come by every so often, only to discover that someone who should have been inside the house, sleeping on his own comfortable Tempurpedic bed, was now occupying their little wooden bench. That was the night it finally dawned on me that life with my foster parents was unraveling and there was no way for me to amend the situation.

The following morning, I was hoping that my foster mother would at least let me inside the house so that I could eat breakfast and get ready for school. However, she locked all the doors and went off to school, leaving me behind. After a while, the hunger became unbearable, so I went by Mr. and Mrs. Lee's house for food. Although Mr. and Mrs. Lee had five children and had no real source of income, those limitations did not stop them from offering me food and shelter. I ended up staying with them for the remainder of the day. Later that evening, I went home but was once again greeted by my foster mother's barrage of crude and humiliating remarks. She concluded by saying, "Don't even think about putting your foot inside my house." With that, I had no other choice but to spend the rest of the week with the Lee family.

The neighbors informed Mr. and Mrs. Lee that they were not permitted to take me into their home without the consent of the CDA. This statement is similar to the legal warning you would hear during a sporting event; the one which states, "This transmission cannot be reproduced or be retransmitted without the written consent of the NBA." In my case, this legal disclaimer could be read as, "Desmond cannot be adopted or fostered without the written consent of the CDA." As dramatic as it may sound, that was the CDA's policy. With that said, Mr. and Mrs. Lee had no other choice but to provide me with a legal basis as to why they were not permitted to keep me at their home.

After having been away for several days, on December 5, 1983, I finally decided to go back home and apologize to my foster mother. I did not see her, but instead, I saw a little cardboard box that had a couple of pieces of my clothing. Based on my recollection, there were two shirts and one pair of pants. As I stood there gazing at the little cardboard box, my thought process was interrupted when my foster mother came out onto the verandah and, in a stern voice said, "A man yuh a play. Coltie a di only man in here." ("You are pretending to be a man. Coltie is the only man here.") Those were the exact words she had uttered just before she took my brother and dropped him off at the dreaded Copse juvenile correctional institution. Shortly after that, she ordered me to go shower and get dressed, because she was taking me back to the CDA. Right then and there I could see the clear, concise, and compelling writing on the wall; and it revealed that life with my foster parents had come to an end.

The Inevitable

With many obscure thoughts stirring in my mind, I found myself resorting to the "if I had known" wishful thinking. I was thinking that if I had just stayed home, none of this would have happened. Why had I gone off socializing with the neighbor's children without my foster mother's permission? Why and why? At the time, I placed the blame squarely on my childish actions. However, many years later, I found out that socializing with the neighbor's children was not the main reason why my foster parents removed me from their home and took me back to the CDA. I will explain the shocking discovery shortly.

Not having the slightest clue of the whereabouts of my parents or even a distant family member only made my life a lot more complicated. Therefore, I had no other choice but to do exactly as I was told. Immediately after I was through getting dressed, my foster mother escorted me to the vehicle. I was not even allowed to have a cup of hot mint beverage. Okay, let's forget about the hot beverage because I am quite sure that food was never one of the many thoughts that were weighing down my mind that morning. Moreover, I should not have been asking for anything hot because the heat that was being directed at me by my foster mother was far more than I could tolerate.

Despite my added humor, I was experiencing extreme sadness and loneliness that was compounded with a deep sense of desperation. At that defining moment, I was witnessing the final chapter of what I would describe as "The Elusive Life of Coercion and Deception" being fulfilled right before my eyes. The five long years I spent with my foster parents had dwindled down to just a few minutes. On the one hand, I was contemplating the idea of asking for forgiveness with the hope that my foster parents would change their minds. While on the other hand, a compelling voice was telling me just to take my chances and go with the unknown. I chose the latter because I believed that my foster parents had made up their minds and I was no longer welcome in their house. My relationship with my foster parents had reached the point of no return. Right then and there, I knew that I was about to share the same fate as my brother.

So, there I was, sitting in the minivan holding the little cardboard box in my lap while waiting for my foster parents. However, it appeared as though my foster parents deliberately slowed the process to a crawl so that I could have ample time to reflect on the "good life" I was leaving behind. As I sat there reflecting on the past five years, my thoughts were interrupted when my foster parents came into the vehicle and we commenced our journey. Once again, I found myself embarking on yet another adventure that was taking me deeper into life's unknown.

Being Shuttled into the Great Unknown

As I sat in the vehicle and stared into the abyss, my mind was burdened with mixed emotions concerning the unknown. Although I did not know precisely where my foster parents were taking me, having a small window into their minds and remembering what they told me concerning my brother, I could see a dark and lonely road leading to the dreaded Copse juvenile correctional institution. Moreover, the possibility of being taken to such a place had plagued my mind ever since the day my foster parents took my brother there. Copse was always a place that every orphan child dreaded and tried to avoid at all costs. However, based on the events that were unfolding, it appeared as though I had not tried hard enough.

Finally, my foster parents stopped at the CDA office located in Falmouth, Trelawny. My foster mother beckoned to me to come on out of the vehicle. With not much haste, I took the little cardboard box and exited the vehicle as if I were a USPS delivery person. After making the first couple of steps, it felt as though I had stepped off the face of the earth and there was no longer any support beneath me. I am not sure if my feet had fallen asleep or I was merely defying gravity. Of course, nothing was wrong with my feet, but instead, it was the extreme nervousness and anxiety that were affecting my mobility.

Back in the Hands of the Child Development Agency

Despite the overwhelming anxiety, I managed to walk up the steps and into the CDA office. The minute we walked through the door, I could detect that the two CDA representatives were looking a bit perplexed, as if we were unwelcome guests. Moreover, witnessing a child being escorted into the building by his foster parents was definitely not the way they wanted to start out their workweek.

Trying not to make matters worse, I stood off to the side and kept really quiet while my foster parents, more so my foster mother, did all the talking. Well, it was more like complaining bitterly. She had a brief, but stern discussion with the CDA representatives. Ladies and gentlemen of the jury, I was brought up on three charges: First, my foster mother told the CDA officers that I had run away from home and was sleeping out at nights. Second, she told them that I had stolen hundreds of dollars they had saved by switching to Geico. Well, except for the Geico part, stealing hundreds of dollars from their possessions was one of the charges that were levied against me. Third—here comes the "waiting to exhale" breath-stopper accusation—she told the officers that I was sleeping with all of the girls who were residing at her home.

My first internal reaction was, all of the girls! All of them! I guess she had to exaggerate her claim so that the CDA officers would have no other choice but to recommend that I be transferred to Copse. In hindsight, I wonder what Joy, Ann, Carol, Debby, Totlyn, Jacqueline, and the other boarders would have had to say about this. Wow! Now I was in a lot more trouble than I had originally thought. I was going to need a high-powered attorney to defend me against these serious charges, especially the third.

My brother was brought up on two charges, which included not obeying the rules and running away from home, and for those charges, he was taken to the juvenile correctional institution. So if he were taken to such a place, then can you imagine what my fate was going to be when the final judgment was handed down? Looking back, I am very lucky that Guantanamo Bay detention camp was not one of the choices that were made available to my foster parents. If so, then I would have been the first juvenile to be shipped off to Gitmo. On a more somber note, my foster mother's whole intention was to make sure that George and I ended up at places where we would be isolated and would, most likely, not experience normal lives.

After my foster mother was through levying the charges against me, Ms. Davis, one of the CDA officers, turned to me and said, "Desmond there is no available space in any of the orphanages, so my advice to you is that you apologize to your foster parents so that they might consider taking you back." Immediately, my foster mother interrupted Ms. Davis and said, "That is not an option! It's too late for an apology! No matter how many times he apologizes, he is not coming back!" Every time that I review this section, it reminds me of OneRepublic's dismal lyrics, "It's too late to apologize."

When I heard those words, tears began to flow down my cheeks. This was the first time in my life that I had found myself crying uncontrollably and not being punished physically. After witnessing my crying, my foster mother started levying all sorts of condescending remarks at me. Finally, after she was through mocking me, she looked directly at me and said, "It is too late for your tears, you should have thought about your actions before going off behaving like you are the man of the house." In hindsight, I should have asked my foster mother how many of us had she accusing of vying for the "man of the house" title! First, it was Roy, then Barry, then Phillip (well, she had some legitimacy with regard to Phillip), then Maxwell, then my brother, and finally me. I wonder why the girls had never been accused of acting as though they were the woman of the house. Okay moving on.

I remember Ms. Davis looked directly at my foster mother and said, "If Desmond was stealing hundreds of dollars from your possession, did you not see anything tangible that he was spending that much money on?" In this instance, Ms. Davis was simply trying to uncover the reason why a child would need that much money. I could sense that my foster mother was irritated that she was being questioned by the CDA officer. Not only that, but she was unable to substantiate her claim, so she turned to Ms. Davis and said, "Desmond is a big gambler, he gambled away my money." After hearing such a response, Ms. Davis turned to my foster mother and said, "I will handle the situation from here." Immediately after that, my foster mother beckoned to her husband just before she stormed out of the office in a rage.

Before I bring this foster care experience to a close, I would like to make a point based on my observations concerning my former foster parents. After putting everything into perspective, I firmly believe that my foster mother had to have been suffering from some form of childhood psychological trauma. My assertion was based on the remarks she would utter while she was punishing my brother and me. I distinctly remember on several occasions, after she was through beating us, she would say, "Yes, man! When I was a little girl and my father was beating me, a little old man who lived next door would come by the fence and say to my father, 'Laud massa! Save her skin to make drums.'" ("Lord Mister! . . .") I believe the "little old man" was attempting to get the attention of my foster mother's father to let him know that he did not approve of his abusive behavior.

The next action that revealed my foster mother's childhood trauma was when she threw an object and hit us and then reminded us that her father would do the same to her. Her actual words were, "Yes, man! When a cawn season mi haffi stay up all nite an shell cawn, an when mi fall asleep, mi fada woulda tek one a di biggest cawn and nak mi inna mi head." ("Yes, man! When it was corn season, I had to stay up all night shucking and shelling corn, and when I fell asleep, my father would throw one of the biggest corns and hit me on the head.") In this regard, she was justifying her actions by letting us know that she had suffered similar punishment at the hand of her father throughout her childhood years. For the five years I spent with my foster mother, she never had anything positive to say regarding her father.

While I do not mind parents exercising strict discipline, I believe that they should not punish or abuse a child to justify their pasts. Abuse, whether it be physical or psychological, should not continue from one generation to the next. It is not DNA. Nor is it innate. It is a behavior that can be corrected. However, it requires admission. I wish my foster mother had a way of knowing that she needed psychological help and had sought counseling in such regard. The same goes for my foster father even though he was not responsible for most of the abuse. At times it may seem easier for us parents to do all the talking, yelling, or beating, but I would suggest that we also give a listening ear to our children. Even with my first-hand experience, I have to keep reminding myself not to adopt my foster parents' regimented parenting approach. Throughout our childhood years, my brother and I lived in fear and constant humiliation because of the physical and psychological abuse we endured at the hands of our foster parents. This lifestyle severely hindered our ability to communicate with our foster parents and, even at times, with others.

Regardless of how painful it has been for me to write this volume, I can assure you that it has helped me to understand and to put in context why George was always reminding our foster parents (more so our foster mother) that their treatment toward us was unjust.

Irrespective of everything that took place over the five years that I lived with my former foster parents, I believe that they came to terms with their harmful actions in their later years. I am not alone in this regard, because in one of my conversations with Christopher many years later, he concluded likewise. I was relieved when he told me that he had not received any of the inhumane treatment that the foster children had experienced. Christopher was the only child who had been born and raised in the care of my foster parents. Therefore, he had an opportunity to bond with them emotionally, which is something the foster children, and most likely, her adopted children never experienced. To have learned that my former foster parents have changed, has brought closures to a very painful chapter of my childhood. However, it took too many years, and the scarring of the lives of too many children, before they realized that what they were doing was wrong. I believe that there is a strong probability that my foster parents could have made this change earlier had we stood up collectively and made it known to them that their actions toward the children were immoral. In this regard I am holding myself accountable because I did not stand in solidarity with my brother in his pursuit of justice. I have fallen short because I could only see the tangible things that benefited me.

Thank you very much for choosing to read volume 2 of my autobiography. I hope you have found the first phase of my foster care experience informative and, at times, compelling. Although this volume has painted the darker side of my foster care experience, I hope my tidbit sense of humor bring out a few smiles and even caused you to chuckle a few times as well. If you wish to explore the second phase of my foster care experience, please proceed to volume 3 of my autobiography.

JAMAICA - THE JOURNEY

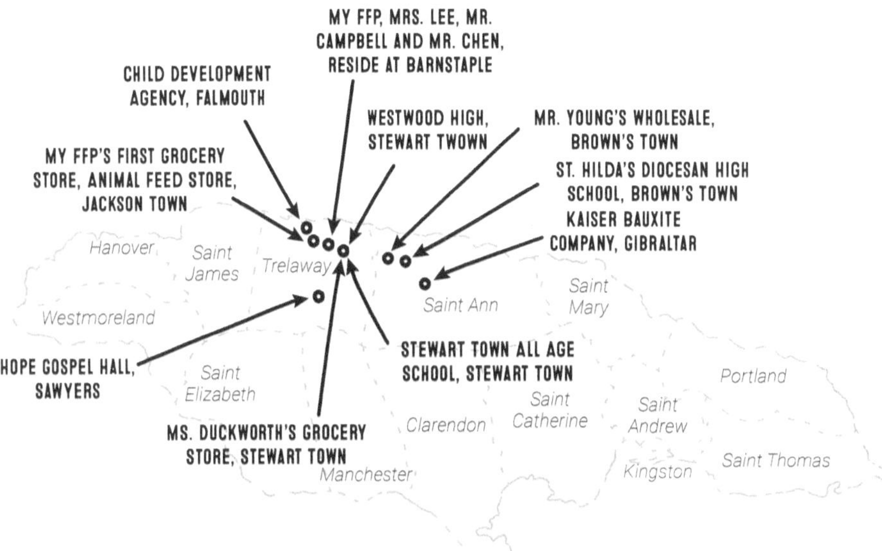

"FFP" signifies *Former Foster Parents*

PREDATED AND POSTDATED ERAS OF THE FOSTER CARE SYSTEM

I would like to share with you a brief overview of my findings as they relate to the actions taken on behalf of orphans and abandoned children in the predated (prior to the mid-19th century) and postdated (the mid-20th century and beyond) eras of the foster care system. This research is to uncover the progress made since the advent of the foster care system. I have also used my foster care experience to highlight similarities with the findings documented by the articles outlined below. Finally, I have included a few statistics to provide a more quantifiable view of the foster care systems in Jamaica and the United States.

According to the Merriam Webster dictionary, foster care is a process that involves "a situation in which for a period of time a child lives with and is cared for by people who are not the child's parents." The Child Protection and Family Services Agency (CPFSA) of Jamaica defines foster care as "a process that places a child in the care of a person or couple who are not the biological parents of the child, to enable them to raise that child and provide a nurturing environment for his or her physical, spiritual and emotional growth and development." ("Foster Care FAQ"). The agency also states that "Foster Care is aimed at providing a safe family haven for children under 18 years who have become wards of the state as a result of being abused, orphaned, abandoned, neglected or because of the inability of parents, relatives or guardians to care for them." (The Child Protection and Family Services Agency (CPFSA) 2019). According to the Department of Children and Families "Foster Care means care provided for a foster child by a person licensed, approved or certified to provide such care." ("DEFINITIONS").

Just by reading the definitions of foster care, one would conclude that the actions taken by the foster parents have always reflected the system's creed. That is, to love and care for the child or children as any loving and caring parent or parents would do unto their own. Based on evidence compiled in the article, "What We Know about the Effects of Foster Care," however, social work faculty at the Institute for Research on Poverty at the University of Wisconsin-Madison stated that "Unprotected children have not fared well over the course of history." Around the Middle Ages, churches and workhouses became an alternative to the popular practices of infanticide and abandonment. Before the advent of Foster Care and appropriate laws, "older children had some economic value for the work they could perform, they were indentured. Indeed, they were not considered children, but rather small adults as far as work was concerned, except they had none of the rights of adults." The authors went on to say, "In Tudor England, children reached the age of majority at nine" (McDonald et al. 22).

The synopsis outlined above is just one of many articles that help to paint a dismal picture of the lives of orphans and abandoned children prior to the advent of the foster care system. In contrast, the lives of children following the advent of the foster care system have improved significantly, but the system had issues because of the foster parents' perceived self-interest. The first well-known foster family care program in the United States was the placing-out system of the New York Children's Aid Society. This program was established by Charles Loring Brace in 1853, with the goal of disposing of vagrant children. Children were rounded up from the city streets and obtained from institutions and shipped to rural communities in the West or South, where committees of citizens arranged for them to be taken in by families. A description of the procedure makes it sound like a slave auction, and it was generally conceded that the motives of the families with whom the children were placed had more to do with self-interest than Christian charity (McDonald et al. 22).

It is quite clear that although the original intent of the system was for a noble cause, the recipients of the orphan children viewed the foster care system as an opportunity to serve their own interests rather than the well-being of the children. Although not as severe, this process was similar to the workhouse concept that was practiced in the United Kingdom. However, as bodies such as the United Nations, in its Declaration of the Rights of the Child (1959) and Convention on the Rights of the Child (1998) and the Pew Commission began to be heard, the well-being of children worldwide improved significantly. Also, programs implemented by many government agencies such as the Children's Bureau (a subdivision of U.S.

Department of Health and Human Services) focus on improving the lives of children and families through a variety of programs.

According to a study commissioned by UNICEF in partnership with the Planning Institute of Jamaica, poverty is one of the many reasons why many children ended up in the foster care system. The study stated that the total number of Jamaican children in poverty just ten years ago was 170,004 (Witter, Hamil, and Spencer 2009, 47). According to another study, "A Study of the Foster Care Programme in Jamaica," by the end of December 2007, there were 2,442 children in institutional care in Jamaica, of which 1,160 were in foster care (Malcolm 2012). In the United States of America, there were 437,283 children in foster care, per the 2018 AFCARS report, which cited neglect and parental drug abuse as the two major contributing factors why children ended up in foster care. Data from the American Institutes for Research shows that poverty and homelessness are also significant contributors. A recent article on their website reveals, "A staggering 2.5 million children are now homeless each year in America. This historic high represents one in every 30 children in the United States" (Bassuk, et al. 2018).

Unintended Consequences of the Foster Care System

Whether the child is "placed with a family member, relatives or strangers, in a group home, or in an institution whatever its form, foster care is an enormous upheaval in the life of a child," the Institute for Research on Poverty has found. The child "must adjust not only to a different family, a different location, a different school, and different peers, but to a different culture as well (McDonald, et al. 22). My brother and I have experienced the emotional and psychological effects of these unpredictable upheavals, which I have documented throughout the four volumes that constitute my autobiography.

The current state of the foster care system, the findings highlighted by above articles, and my foster care experience have revealed the obvious, which is that there is still more work to be done to educate the public, especially prospective foster parents, to ensure that there is a clear, unambiguous understanding concerning the true meaning of fostering. In other words, we need to recognize and understand that the well-being of the child is our most important priority.

It is with this understanding that I would also like to broaden the concept of fostering by introducing the word "fostership." Although fostership is not a formally defined word, I believe that it emphasizes the relationship a person should embrace when considering becoming a foster parent. In this context, "fostership" does not only apply to the process of removing a child from the streets, orphanage, or from his or her biological family with the sole intention of placing him or her into a foster home. Instead, it is an everyday caring and nurturing commitment for the parent or parents, teachers, pastors, institutions, and other affiliations that the child may encounter as he or she progresses through life. With that said, I would like to define fostering as follows: Fostering is an everyday commitment assumed by all responsible parties to promote the well-being of a person, especially that of the child. Throughout the four volumes that constitute my autobiography, I have used my experiences to compare and contrast the differences between fostering as a mere process (one that is mostly driven by selfish desires) and fostering (fostership) that has been established through a *compassionate* and *loving* relationship. I emphasized the words compassionate and loving because when fused together they become the precursor for meaningful parent-child relationships.

I was very fortunate because my second foster parent, Fredricka Lucy Brady (Aunt Lucy), allowed me to enjoy a wonderful foster-parent/foster-child relationship. This experience is why I strongly recommend that everything should be done to identify and deny individuals such as my former foster parents the opportunity to adopt, foster, or become the legal guardians of a child.

Additional sources

- https://fosteringthroughtheeyesofachild.net/
- https://www.childwelfare.gov/pubPDFs/f_fospar.pdf
- https://www.childwelfare.gov/pubPDFs/extensionfc.pdf
- https://www.acf.hhs.gov/cb
- https://www.irp.wisc.edu/publications/focus/pdfs/foc142g.pdf
- http://www.welcome.oca.gov.jm/
- https://www.unicef.org/jamaica/Foster_Care_in_Jamaica.pdf
- https://www.acf.hhs.gov/sites/default/files/cb/afcarsreport26.pdf

- http://www.ohchr.org/EN/ProfessionalInterest/Pages/CRC.aspx
- http://www.pewtrusts.org/en/archived-projects/commission-on-children-in-foster-care
- http://www.childrensrights.org/issues-resources/foster-care/facts-about-foster-care/
- http://www.myflfamilies.com/service-programs/independent-living/myfuturemychoice-fp

A PAINFUL LESSON

One of my regular routines was to take my children to the doctor. On my way to the doctor's office, I usually stopped at the rest area to allow my younger daughter to go to the restroom. On this particular day, she was sleeping, so I woke her and told her to accompany me to the restroom. However, she told me that she did not need to use the restroom and immediately went back to sleep. With that said, I told my sixteen-year-old daughter to keep watch while I went to the restroom. I was pressed for time, so after I was through, I went directly to the car and continued on my journey.

What I did not realize was that my younger daughter had exited the vehicle and gone into the restroom. Immediately, after discovering that she was not in the car, I felt as though I was experiencing my worst nightmare. The only place that she could possibly be was at the rest area where we had stopped, which was approximately twenty to twenty-five minutes' drive. I can assure you that this twenty-five-minute drive appeared to be the longest distance I ever have driven in my entire life! It felt as though my destination was located at the end of eternity!

However, my nerves were calmed when I received a phone call, and the person on the line told me that my daughter was with him and that she was safe. As soon as I arrived at the rest area, I hurried to where my daughter was and embraced her passionately. Just to know that she was in my arms and that I was able to embrace her was a life experience that I am unable to explain with words. After thanking the sheriff and the couple who had taken care of my daughter, I picked her up and took her to the car, forgetting that she could walk. Even to this day, I still do not know why I did not let her walk to the car. Prior to this experience, I always asked myself if I really love my children enough. However, I can assure you that this experience put to rest the lingering fear that I had regarding my childhood circumstances' preventing me from loving my children the way they should be loved.

Picking up my child from the rest area was not the end of this unfortunate experience. My wife and I had to undergo a lengthy process of cross-examination by the Department of Children and Families (DCF) to prove that we were responsible parents. My children were questioned privately as well. This was the most devastating period in my adult life, especially knowing that the likelihood of my children being removed from my care was real! This whole process terrified me because it brought back painful memories of the many instances in which my siblings and I had been forcefully removed from our parents' care, divvied up, and transferred to orphanages and foster homes. I can only imagine the emotional pain my parents must have endured when we were forcefully removed from their care.

However, this process was necessary because due diligence must be done and should not be assumed by those in authority. Moreover, this is the very outcome I advocate for in my autobiography and also stressed to the Child Development Agency (CDA) representatives of Jamaica. After all the things that I have been through in life, especially those throughout my childhood years, I would have never imagined that someday I would be asked to prove that I was a responsible parent.

Although this was a painful experience for me, I have viewed it as one that I can use to help others, more so parents and prospective parents. With that said, here is my advice to all parents and legal guardians: First, please make sure that you are aware of where your children are at all times and that they are in responsible hands if they are not physically in your presence. Second, please never assume (as I did) that where you left a child is where you will find the child. Please make sure that your children are accounted for before, during, and at the end of your journey.

JAMAICAN, ACADEMIC LEVELS, PROGRESS, AND INSTITUTIONS

Throughout my primary school years (1979–1982), the Common Entrance Exam (no longer available today) provided students who were enrolled in the fifth and sixth grades the opportunity to pursue the high school track. If successful, the student would earn a place in one of the many high schools across the island. If the student was not successful on the Common Entrance Exam or simply was not given such an opportunity (as it was in the case of the other foster children), then at age thirteen, the student would have the opportunity to pursue the Technical Entrance or the Grade Nine Achievement academic track. If they were not so fortunate to take advantage of any of the above opportunities (which was the case for the majority of the students from the poorer communities), then such students would have to complete their secondary academic careers at one of the many all-age or vocational institutions

I would also like to point out three reasons why attending high school was not an affordable option for everyone. First, the high school entrance exam process was a very costly undertaking because the students had to attend many hours of preparatory/prep classes over one year before being allowed to sit the exam. Also, the child's parent or parents would be responsible for the total costs associated with the afterschool class sessions. Second, the student had only two tries to obtain a passing grade on the entrance exam, similar to a "two strikes and you are out" rule. Third, only a very small percentage of the qualified students from a given primary or all-age were allowed to sit the high school entrance exam, as was the case for the Stewart Town All-Age School I attended. school were allowed to sit the high school entrance exam, as was the case for the Stewart Town All-Age School I attended.

Resources regarding the more recent education system can be found at the following sites:

http://www.moe.gov.jm/
https://www.cxc.org/
http://www.classbase.com/Countries/Jamaica/
    Education-System
http://www.heart-nta.org/

Also, for an overview of the United States' education system, please visit:

https://www.ed.gov/

REFERENCES

"The AFCARS Report: Preliminary FY[1] 2018 Estimates as of August 22, 2019," No. 26, U.S. Department of Health and Human Services, 22 Aug. 2019, https://www.acf.hhs.gov/sites/default/files/cb/afcarsreport26.pdf.

Bassuk, Ellen L., Carmela J. DeCandia, Corey Anne Beach, and Fred Berman. "America's Youngest Outcasts: A Report Card on Child Homelessness." *American Institutes for Research*, The National Center on Family Homelessness, 27 Sept. 2018, https://www.air.org/resource/americas-youngest-outcasts-report-card-child-homelessness.

"DEFINITIONS." *CT.gov*, Department of Children and Families, accessed 21 Nov. 2019. https://portal.ct.gov/DCF/1-DCF/Commonly-Used-DCF-Words-Phrases.

"Foster Care." *ACF*, The Children's Bureau, 9 Aug. 2019, https://www.acf.hhs.gov/cb/focus-areas/foster-care.

"Foster Care FAQ." *Protecting Children, Empowering Families, Securing the Future*, The Child Protection and Family Services Agency (CPFSA), accessed 10 Nov. 2019. http://childprotection.gov.jm/foster-care/foster-care-faq/.

Malcolm, Rodje. "Jamaica—A Study of Foster Care in Jamaica," Office of the Children's Advocate, *LinkedIn*

SlideShare, 21 Dec. 2012, https://www.slideshare.net/rodjemalcolm/oca-foster-care-in-jamaica.

McDonald, Thomas, Reva Allen, Alex Westerfelt, and Irving Piliavin. "Assessing the Long-Term Effects of Foster Care: A Research Synthesis." *What We Know about the Effects of Foster Care*, IRP Special Report, accessed 10 Nov. 2019. https://www.irp.wisc.edu/publications/focus/pdfs/foc142g.pdf.

Reynolds, Ras Dennis Jabari. *Jabari Authentic Jamaican Dictionary of the Jamic Language Featuring, Jamaican Patwa and Rasta Iyaric, Pronunciations and Definitions.* Around the Way Books, 2006.

Williams, Petre. "'They Beat Us Here'." *Jamaica Observer*, 19 June 2005, http://www.jamaicaobserver.com/news/'They-beat-us-here'.

Witter, Michael, Kelly-Ann Dixon Hamil, and Nekeisha Spencer. *Child Poverty and Disparities in Jamaica.* UNICEF, Jamaica and the Planning Instiute of Jamaica, 9 Oct. 2009, https://www.unicef.org/socialpolicy/files/Jamaica_Child_Poverty_and_Disparity.pdf.